YOUR BRAIN:
FRIEND & FOE

---

7 Keys to reduce self-sabotage
and become more successful

GAIL PEMBERTON

Published by KHARIS PUBLISHING, imprint of KHARIS MEDIA LLC.

Copyright © 2020 Gail Pemberton

ISBN-13: 978-1-946277-44-2
ISBN-10: 1-946277-44-4

All KHARIS PUBLISHING products are available at special quantity discounts for bulk purchase for sales promotions, premiums, fund-raising, and educational needs. For details, contact:

Kharis Media LLC
Tel: 1-479-599-8657
support@kharispublishing.com
www.kharispublishing.com

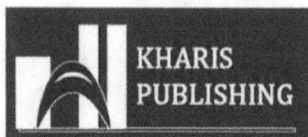
KHARIS PUBLISHING

PRAISE FOR
YOUR BRAIN: FRIEND & FOE

I have known Gail Pemberton for 25 years, first as my student in graduate-level psychotherapy, then as a clinical supervisee, and now as a respected and deeply appreciated colleague.

Throughout this time, Gail has shown a steady, deep and passionate commitment to knowing herself and all her relationships better, psychologically and spiritually.

Gail walks her talk, and her book reflects her hard-won wisdom and experience in her personal and professional life.

This book is very readable, and yet has a strong underlying structure based on sound psychological principles, clinical experience, and research findings. Gail's skills, and integrity, in conveying subtle and sophisticated psychological knowledge in a most readable fashion are remarkable

> – *Michael Le Page, Ph.D. Clinical Psychologist in private practice, Sydney, Australia Former lecturer in clinical psychology, California State University-Hayward CA; Dominican University, San Rafael CA.*

***

Gail Pemberton's decades of clinical experience as an Individual and Couples Therapist help us understand the multilayered aspects of our relationships to ourselves and others.

With her meaningful anecdotes Gail challenges the reader to recognize the power emotions have over us and how complex dynamics between our unconscious, instinctual reactions affect our relationships. Her many useful examples and self-check questions demonstrate that, by looking first at ourselves, we can create healthier connections with our partner, children, family, friends and colleagues.

I highly recommend this well-structured, practical and easy to follow self-help book.

> – *Yolanda Waldman M. Analytical Psychology Lecturer at JNI (part of Laureate University USA)*

***

Gail Pemberton is an insightful academic, researcher and communicator. Her latest book *Your Brain-Friend and Foe* is an excellent example of these qualities.

She demystifies the complexities of the brain on human behavior using everyday language with clarity and humor. An informative read with great practical advice.

– Honorable Susan Lenehan Former Minister of Education (South Australia)

***

If you're curious about the neuroscience and psychology which sits behind how to create and sustain healthy relationships, then I highly endorse author, Gail Pemberton. In my 25 years of experience working with Executives and MBA students, I've seldom run across such practical advice and evidence-based guidelines on how to ensure successful relationships.

This is essential reading and I recommend Gail's book to all of my graduate students and clients.

– Denise Weinreis Australian Graduate School of Management (AGSM) FellowAdjunct Associate Professor at the University of New South Wales Business School Sydney, Australia

***

Pemberton's latest book *Your Brain – Friend and Foe* follows on from her previous publication *The Brain's Business*. This time, the focus has shifted from a business orientation to personal relationships. Pemberton argues that we navigate life heavily influenced by programming from early childhood. She also shows how seemingly mundane or meaningless changes can greatly impact our behavior when we don't realize what's going on, which appears to be a majority of the time.

This book also has some meaningful insights on relationship management. I'm recommending it because it's an insightful look at how to avoid projection and retool our approach to "problematic" people for more successful and rewarding personal relationships.

– Professor Steve Burdon AM, FIEA, FAICD, FIML Professor of Strategic Management & Technology, UTS

CONTENTS

INTRODUCTION

"Our brains are up to more than we think and it's not all good ... we can and often are sabotaging ourselves without even realising it."

H e turns on his heel, stamps out of the room yelling: "I'm jack of this, I'm out of here." She sinks down onto the chair, head in hands and starts sobbing. Is this relationship a fiasco or self-sabotage or both? What just happened?

His crocodile brain took over. What? What's a crocodile brain?

Our crocodile brain is the largest part of our brain, usually called the unconscious or the subconscious. Your unconscious influences all your behavior, beliefs, and thoughts, yet we are largely unaware of its presence, let alone its power. It impacts every emotion we have and fuels our every motivation. Few of us even know about it, yet there it is working away in everyone's brain, generally causing chaos.

I use the term the unconscious (as it is the term that is generally used by professionals, talking about mental functioning. [1]), but you may like to think of it as the subconscious. This will be discussed extensively later.

Whatever you want to call it, the unconscious can and generally does cause havoc with our relationships. As you read on you will understand why. In fact, I thought of calling this book *Is Your Brain Hijacking Your Relationships?* But decided that *Your Brain – Friend And Foe* was a fairer way of looking at this magnificent organ. Because, the brain is indeed magnificent. Your brain can process between 11

---

1   Harvard Health Publication www.health.harvard.edu/blog/unconscious-or-subconscious-20100801255

million and 40 million pieces of information per second. That is an amazing fact, and no doubt as science learns more that number will increase. But we come to all this later.

"I don't have a magic wand, and neither does your doctor, therapist, psychic, best friend or mother... However, the benefit will change your life."

***

For now, let's cut to the chase. I'm going to be brutally honest; I'm not going to butter you up with wild promises ... that you will never self-sabotage or never hijack your own relationships.

My goal is to give you the tools that we as psychotherapists, psychologists, and doctors took years to learn. I've distilled countless studies, proven theories, and decades of experience into 7 key learnings, that have the power to transform your relationships into something better. And we start with the most important relationship of all, yourself. But, I warn you up front, it will be hard work, so if that frightens you, stop reading now. I wish I could say it'll be easy but this work of changing your life demands focus, awareness and commitment. However, the benefit will change your life.

I don't have a magic wand, and neither does your doctor, therapist, psychic, best friend or mother. There's no magic fairy dust to sprinkle over you, to make it all perfect, relationship strife disappears, and we live happily ever after.

BUT... despite the apparent lack of 'abracadabra', I do have tools and information that will start to transform your relationships and help you understand yourself, and by default, the other people in your life. In fact, it will turn into abracadabra, because abracadabra means, "I will create as I speak" in Aramaic. Awareness from this book will help you weave magic through your life and relationships.

It all boils down to 7 well-known, proven psychological facts, backed by neuroscience. We have all heard about neuroscience, but we don't necessarily know what impact it has on us. As we go on, I will link the 7 keys back to simple neuroscience so you get a better idea.

"What I discovered, is that our issues and needs all boil down to being very similar, whether we are the head of a top 100 listed company, or somebody coming out of jail."

***

The bad news is that, while you can do all the hard work and change yourself, you can't change the people that you are in relationship with. However, by understanding these well-known and proven psychological facts, your life does get better. And the payoff is when you make changes, others also change. You won't shoot yourself in the foot so often. You will be able to work out what could be going wrong and the rest becomes easier to resolve.

The problem is that relationship problems don't just magically happen and conversely, they don't just magically go away. However, it helps when you start to appreciate what is going on behind the scenes, in the way your brain evolved.

What I learned on my own journey of self-discovery, was that it wasn't about blaming others and wanting them to change, which was always what I did and unfortunately still tend to do - even after nearly 35 years of learning about this stuff. It was about understanding why I thought the way I did, and how my own unique programming had influenced the way I choose to see things. This information was so profound for me that I wrote You Can Live with Anyone, well almost, in order to pass it on.

Much of the information in this short book is distilled from that earlier book, You Can Live with Anyone, well almost, which evolved from many years of practical experience, dealing with thousands of people with many different types of problems. What I discovered, is that our issues and needs all boil down to being very similar, whether we are the head of a top 100 listed company, or somebody coming out of jail.

We need food, shelter, and we received programming from our parents or caregivers as children. This programming forms the basis of our beliefs and perceptions about the world and ourselves. From there, we go on to have relationships and this is usually where the difficulties start.

"With all the experts effectively saying the same thing, it behoves us to look at this cutting-edge information and be early adopters. The result is improved lives."

***

Underlying all human interactions are the 7 psychological keys. Once we have a handle on these, change begins. You will understand how you can make conscious choices. Believe it or not, while we may think we are in control most of the time we are not, and I'll show you why.

Your work will improve your relationships and as Dr. Louis Cozolino says in his book, *The Healthy Aging Brain*,[2] how well we age depends on the quality of our relationships. When you think of the amount of time you spend interacting with others, it pays to make those relationships easier, more effective, and stimulating. Dr. Dan Siegel, another expert neuroscientist, says: "Our behavior impacts our brain physiology. We know that experiences shape the brain throughout life by altering the connections among neurons".[3] This work changes your brain.

"Moment to moment our choices change the functioning of our brain and impact the way we see the world and interact with it," says Dr. David Rock, one of the thought leaders in human performance.[4] With all the experts effectively saying the same thing, it behoves us to look at this cutting-edge information and be early adopters. The result is improved lives.

Over the years my clients have said, "I wish I had known this earlier. It would have made such a difference to how I handled some difficult situations that I know have impacted my relationships and my career."

***

The Brain's Business - Psychology and Neuroscience for Exceptional Leadership, was the forerunner of this book. It gives much of the same information, but is adapted for the corporate market, where I do a lot of executive education and coaching.

I originally started my career in finance as an investment analyst, and later a financial journalist. I then had my three children and later went back to study psychotherapy where I discovered my passion. Today I teach psychotherapy students at Master's level, work in the

---

2   Dr. Louis Cozolino, *The Healthy Aging Brain* (Professor, Department of Psychiatry and Behavioral Science, University of Washington, School of Medicine).

3   Dr. Dan Siegel, *Pocket Guide to Interpersonal Neurobiology* (Clinical Professor at UCLA School of Medicine).

4   Jeff Schwartz, talking to Dr. David Rock about 'Managing with the Brain in Mind'.

corporate arena, and run a private practise. I love my work and find our psyche fascinating, which is what I want to share with you.

This book will introduce you to your amazing brain and give you the following overview:

- How extraordinary your brain is – the power of your unconscious
- How your brain was and continues to be programmed
- How it can sabotage you without you even realising it – until later
- How to work more effectively in your life with the resultant impact on relationships both socially and at work
- Most importantly, how you can be the best you can be in your relationships

On the next page a brief look at the vital 7 steps that form the foundation of this work and will yield tangible results. Don't worry if you don't quite understand them now, because you will, once they are explained.

Throughout the book there are numerous examples to illustrate each of the keys. At the end of the book are two appendices that look at the 7 keys to empowerment and how the principles fit into our behavior.

At the end of each chapter, I suggest a couple of exercises that will help you in your journey. You would find it helpful to make a note of what springs to mind, as you progress through the book, and your journey unfolds more fully.

7 KEYS

1. All our behavior is initially motivated by 3Ss: Survival, Safety, and Security. Weird I know, but this comes from our crocodile brain, the earliest part of our brain to develop, and the biggest part of our brain. More of this later.

2. Our instinctive drive to protect ourselves and keep safe often causes emotional reactivity and destructive patterns in our relationships.

3. Believe it when I say, our thinking patterns and behavior today remain largely untouched since programming was laid down in early childhood. Unhelpful and unhealthy belief systems are a huge contributor to our self-sabotage.

4. This programming went into the unconscious, and our unconscious influences our every thought and action! (Do you remember learning to drive? There was a lot to master, but now driving is second nature, you don't even think about it, you just do it. Our behavior, attitude, and thinking are like this, embedded into our unconscious.)

5. Our programming taught us to hide what was considered unacceptable behavior, and it sunk into our unconscious - cognitive dissonance in psyche talk.

6. To avoid looking at our own less than perfect characteristics we focus on the faults of others - PROJECTION.

7. Our projections influence the way we think about others and that in turn affects our behavior, often leading to self-sabotage.

CHAPTER 1

Your Crocodile Brain

Our thinking patterns and behavior today remain largely untouched and unnoticed since programming was laid down in early childhood

YOUR CROCODILE BRAIN - as we've already read it's your unconscious. I can hear you ask, 'if it is unconscious how is that going to help me to improve my relationships and my life?' Great question! It all starts with you and understanding yourself, and how our brains are wired.

The following diagram may give you a bit of a jolt because it is a bit frightening looking at the makeup of our brain as a series of cartoons, particularly the horse and the crocodile. If you are anything like me, you pride yourself on being an intelligent thoughtful person, and the idea that a horse and a crocodile may make up parts of our brain is frankly appalling. Unfortunately, it's the truth, but let me explain.

Our whizz-bang, modern day brain actually developed and evolved in three stages. As it evolved, it tacked on new exciting bits capable of higher functioning, but never cleared out the older pre-programmed hardware and this has a nasty habit of sabotaging our more evolved neo-cortex. Think of it like a computer – the hardware is the same and we keep upgrading the software.

The oldest part of our brain is nicknamed the crocodile brain, which developed as we evolved out of the sea; it is the reptilian brain

Our Brain

The newest part of our brain the neo-cortex, the rational part

The second oldest part of the brain - the mammalian brain, the emotional part of unconscious

The oldest part of the brain - the reptilian brain, also part of unconscious

that is the seat of our unconscious, says Cozolini[5] in his book *The Neuroscience of Psychotherapy*. It's still there, of course, and for good reason. Take, for example, a war situation where your survival may depend on you being able to make a split-second decision.

The crocodile brain is good at these split-second decisions, taking just 10 – 50 milliseconds, whereas the more evolved rational brain might just be too slow, putting your survival at risk, taking 500 – 600 milliseconds to make a choice. In lay terms this means your crocodile brain is about half a second faster to process information than our thoughtful neo-cortex.[6] Half a second doesn't sound like much but it is a long time for the brain. While we may not like to think we have a crocodile brain, as part of our brain, it is an unbelievably fast operator.

As we continued to evolve from reptiles to mammals, the next upgrade was our mammalian brain – the limbic system that is the nurturing, caring part of us. As mammals we care for our young, unlike the crocodile who leaves the eggs to hatch and the young to fend for themselves.

---

5   Dr. Louis Cozolini, *The Neuroscience of Psychotherapy*.

6   Dr. Louis Cozolini, *Why Therapy works: Using our minds to change our brains*

Lastly as we stepped from mammals to Homo sapiens, we developed our neo-cortex, our rational thinking part. The part that we like to think of as 'us', the smart, logical, rational person we operate as every day, all day!

Unfortunately, that is not the case; we still use all of our brain hardware and software. Each of the programs are still running but our crocodile brain is often the loudest and most dominant of the lot because it deals with 3 'S' stuff – survival, safety, and security, our first key to improved relationships. We will come to this later in this chapter, because it is absolutely fundamental to understanding our relationships, ourselves, and stopping our self-sabotage.

Unbeknown to us, our crocodile brain takes over in our day-to-day lives, and quite often to our detriment, sabotaging us. Amazing and seemingly ridiculous as this sounds it is the truth.

Our crocodiles largely run our show. Consequently, it is important that we learn to recognise our own individual crocodile, as its decisions will often impact our lives negatively. Let's look at a simple husband and wife example because it is more emotive and shows their crocodile brains more clearly.

A FIGHT

Imagine you and your wife are having an argument about putting out the garbage and it is getting quite heated. Suddenly you are not just shouting about garbage but a whole lot of other things are coming into play, not paying the credit card bill, forgetting her birthday, not noticing that she has changed her hair color, and on it goes.

How did this escalate? What just happened? Your wife's crocodile brain came into play, she had been feeling unsupported for some time and her crocodile was threatened, her security felt undermined, and she was determined things had to change or she was out of the relationship.

It was a fight or flight crocodile moment for her. Now, you were only vaguely aware that things were starting to go off track, so when the fight started you were surprised and startled. Your crocodile went straight into attack and suddenly the situation had escalated dramatically. Your wife was talking of ending the marriage, and your crocodile, reacting out of fear, continued to try and shout her down. This prompted her crocodile to fight harder as well. We have all been in similar situations and reacted irrationally. That's our crocodile, with no sense of rationality, ruling the day and escalating the conflict.*

At a conscious, logical level, of course an argument about garbage is not going to threaten your security, but on a very different level in your brain, your safety and security may indeed feel vulnerable. After all, this may be the umpteenth time she has complained about how she has to nag you to take out the garbage and it may be the last straw in your relationship. She decides she has had enough and wants to end the marriage. Suddenly it's a very different story. Your safety may not be directly threatened, unless she is so angry she picks up the knife she is cutting vegetables with, and lashes out at you, but your security is. Suddenly the assets are going to be split, and where you might have felt a comfort in knowing that the mortgage was being slowly paid off, now the amount you will make from selling the house gets halved. Your security feels halved. It all happens in a second, somewhere deep in your brain, while you are busy arguing about garbage. Feeling vulnerable your brain has triggered the 'fight or flight mechanism' and before you know it, you are yelling even louder, and the situation deteriorates even more. We think we are in control of our lives, but our lives are complex, and until we realise what is going on at a much deeper level we are often just reacting emotionally to a stimulus.

HARDWIRED TO SURVIVE - AND THE 3 'S'S

As humans, and like every other creature in this universe, we are hardwired to survive. Our brains want us to be safe. Fundamentally our brain will do everything it can to keep us alive. We have all read amazing stories about people who have survived phenomenal odds and we gravitate to those stories, asking ourselves – given the circumstances, could we survive too?

On the other hand, stories about people who take their own lives somehow sadden us. The majority of us work extremely hard to preserve our life for as long as possible. Modern medicine is an example of how much our society values 'survival' and not necessarily with a good quality of life.

I wish I was him, he has it all.

Let's look at the 3Ss from an animal's point of view.

Take our crocodile. A crocodile doesn't question whether to 'Survive' or not; he is hardwired to survive in any way he can. To survive he needs food to get strong. Survival isn't the only thing the crocodile needs to do. He needs to be 'Safe' too. He needs to be strong and fierce enough to fend off bigger crocodiles and find a territory. He needs to hunt, rest, and breed, in order to pass on his genes.

If we look at this second 'S', safety, in human terms we have food so we are surviving – the first 'S' is being fulfilled. But we need to find shelter so we are safe from the elements. This is the second 'S'. Shelter will help prevent us being attacked by others, at least we can barricade the door. Back to the crocodile and the last of the 3Ss, 'Security.' The crocodile will feel much more secure when he is the biggest crocodile around, can mate with all the available females and fight off the other crocodiles who want his patch. When all his 3Ss are satisfied he is one happy crocodile.

Back to us, we have food and water so we can survive. We have a house so we have some safety, but now we seek security. We need our job so we can buy our food, pay our mortgage or our rent and be even more secure knowing we have our superannuation. Like the crocodile if we know our larder is full, that we have our house and our job is secure, we can feel we are on the ladder of success.

STATUS - AND THE 3 'S'S

The next step is to ensure that our status, which reflects our 3 'S's, is on view. This might mean a good car, living in the right suburb, going to restaurants, theatres, operas, concerts, having the designer clothes, fancy jewellery, going to fabulous resorts for our holidays, or sending our children to the best schools. These are all signs of status. Our whole industrial world is geared to providing consumers with some level of status, whether it is the smart watch, the great car or having the latest technological gadget.

All sounds simple and obvious but the 3 'S's are essentially fundamental feelings that keep us alive and happy. If at any point we unconsciously feel our survival, our safety or our security is being threatened or endangered we will, and do, react. When one of these 3Ss feels shaky it impacts on our relationships, which can start to go horribly wrong.

It is important to understand that unless our 3 'S's are satisfied we can't move forward to the next step of our own personal evolution, which is to become the very best of who we are, to realise our full potential. These 3 'S's are the pillars that support our higher operating levels.

3 MAIN LEVELS IN THE BRAIN

Another way to think about all this is to understand that there are three main levels of functioning in the brain:

- The conscious mind – our neo-cortex
- The subconscious
- The unconscious – our crocodile brain

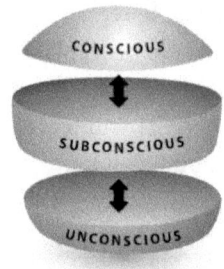

THE CONSCIOUS MIND

This is the newest part of our brain; it evolved after the unconscious and the limbic system. (That is after we evolved from being crocodiles and mammals and into people.)

We all know that the conscious mind is the part that we think with. It is the newest part of our brain, or the most recently evolved, and is called the neo-cortex. The neo-cortex is thought to be more developed in humans than in any other species on the planet. It is the part that thinks, feels, and acts in the present, in the now. It understands time. The conscious mind evaluates, judges, and observes, it looks and sees.

This part of our brain perceives and analyses what is going on and makes decisions based on observations and experiences. We use it to think things through, plan, anticipate, and organise information and ideas. This part of our brain is inherently logical and wants a rational explanation for everything. The conscious mind is orderly and likes to analyse the cause and effect of ideas, thoughts, and actions. The power of criticism also comes from this part of the brain.

The conscious mind is usually used as the gauge in intelligence tests and is the part of the brain that we generally identify with as who we are. Our lives tend to be dominated by it as it rarely shuts up. If you pause for a moment and concentrate on being present, right here in the now, can you shut your thoughts down for a few seconds? For people who haven't tried meditation before this can be a difficult exercise. The power of the conscious mind is so strong that it wants us continually to be thinking some thought.

So, a quick recap on the conscious mind or neo-cortex:
- Newest part of the brain
- Understands time
- Evaluates, judges, and observes
- Looks, sees, and processes
- Perceives, analyses, and makes decisions
- Plans, anticipates, and organises information and ideas
- Essentially logical
- Has the power of criticism
- Is usually the gauge in intelligence tests
- Is the part of the brain we identify with and feel is us

SUBCONSCIOUS

As said earlier, there is a difference between the unconscious and the subconscious. Nowadays the words are used interchangeably, but there are three different levels of consciousness: the conscious, the subconscious, and the unconscious. The unconscious is a deeper level than the subconscious.

The Oxford dictionary definition of the subconscious is: 'being present in consciousness, and capable of being the subject of, or involving, mental activity, but not fully perceived and recognised by the mind, or completely and clearly present to the attention'.

Sounds confusing? Think of it this way – you are walking down the street, past a bookshop, going about your business, and that night you happen to dream of the bookshop and of a particular book in the window. The next day going past the bookshop, you see that the book that you had dreamt of is in the window. You are surprised because the previous day you were not consciously aware of even looking at the window as you passed, yet your subconscious had absorbed that information. The subconscious is not the same powerhouse as the unconscious. You could think of it as the link that goes between consciousness and the unconscious.

THE UNCONSCIOUS

Now we are really getting to the juicy stuff!

The unconscious is the oldest part of the brain. Part of it is made up of the basal ganglia, and it is the unconscious that we are really going to focus on because it plays havoc with our relationships, without us even realising. Sneaky!

Dr Bruce Lipton, an eminent biologist says it is responsible for 95 – 99% of all our actions.[7] So when we think we are being conscious, rational, sensible human beings we are only in that state some 5% of the time. The rest of the time we are reacting to the programming that was laid down in the first six years of our life. Sounds shocking doesn't it? More of this later.

First a quick overview: The unconscious is a collection of modules that operate out of our awareness while we are busy doing other things. For instance, our unconscious enables us to breathe without thinking while simultaneously eating and talking. Our unconscious enables us to function efficiently – it is very smart.

Your unconscious will make the split-second judgement if you are about to do something dangerous, like step in front of a car while day-

---

7   Dr. Bruce Lipton, *The Wisdom of Your Cells*.

dreaming as you walk down the street. It will enable you to recall the name of the high school teacher who was fantastic, but which, until you thought about it, was not in your conscious memory. Likewise, when you are reading a book your unconscious is hard at work helping you instantly recognise words and their meaning and yet you realise that when you go to turn the page that while you have read the words, your thoughts were miles away.

Our unconscious is automatically processing so much of what we do. Remember earlier we talked about driving a car, when we first learned there was so much to think about, now for the majority of us we get into a car and we are "in the zone". Like athletes, musicians, artists and any other profession, when we become unconsciously skilled, as opposed to consciously skilled we can operate at our optimum. We are in the 'flow'.

The defining feature of the unconscious is our ability to operate on automatic pilot. It has five key characteristics. It is:

- Non-conscious
- Fast
- Unintentional
- Uncontrollable
- Effortless

All extremely valuable attributes when used in the appropriate place. We learn so much out of conscious awareness, like when we first learned to talk as children. We were not aware of our learning; it just went into our memory. One of the most important functions of the unconscious is that it absorbs information that threatens our survival faster and better than our conscious minds.

The unconscious is designed to scan the environment quickly and detect patterns easily. However, on the flip side it does not like modifying or changing what it knows, even when it is blatantly incorrect. It is a fairly rigid, inflexible inference-maker. It develops early and continues to guide behavior into adulthood, says Professor Timothy Wilson in his book, *Strangers to Ourselves: Discovering the Adaptive Unconscious.*[8]

---

8   Professor Timothy Wilson, *Strangers to Ourselves: Discovering the Adaptive Unconscious.*

INSTANT DECISIONS - OFTEN OUT OF OUR CONTROL

For example, our unconscious makes an instant decision when we first meet someone, friend or foe? Do I warm to them or feel cool and distant? Problem is once the unconscious has made up its mind it is very difficult to change. It seems we are hardwired to fit people into categories and leave them there.

If the unconscious has decided that someone is a threat, chances are that you will feel uncomfortable around them; Most of the time we don't stop to question that judgement or consciously try and work out why we don't like them. The big disadvantage is that, being set in its habits, our unconscious is slow to respond to new contradictory information, and this is where many of our problems with others arise and we can sabotage ourselves.

Here's the scary part. Even though we believe we are very much in control of our thoughts and actions, it is actually the unconscious that is responsible for some 95 – 99% of our behaviors. I know I am repeating myself, but I feel this astonishing fact bears repeating, because it's a fairly terrifying thought - we don't actually have much idea of what goes on in our unconscious at all!

If I asked you what your unconscious is processing at this very moment, I bet you would be surprised. Besides being responsible for virtually every thought and action we have, our unconscious amazingly processes about 11 million pieces of information per second.

Yes, you read that right – 11 million pieces of information per second, of which we can only be consciously aware of about 40. How staggering is that? In fact, that 11 million has now been superseded by new research by Dr Lipton that says every second the subconscious (or unconscious in our terminology), is processing some 40 million pieces of information per second. Our unconscious is a million times more powerful as an information processor than our conscious mind. Less than 5% of our neural activity is influenced or controlled by our conscious mind.

Even thinking about registering 40 pieces of information per second you would still need to be unbelievably aware, perhaps of your breath, of your shoe holding your foot, the moistness of your lips etc. I can only be aware of about 10 as a maximum before I start losing track. But that is how brilliant our unconscious is.

Admittedly, about 10 million of those pieces of information processed per second come from our ability to see, so we are processing and analysing what our eyes are recording. The remaining 30 million are all the chemical and electrical signals we are sending and receiving by all the 50 trillion cells that make up our body. So, 95% of the time I am operating out of my neurological system based on my unconscious programming and perceptions.

Before you start condemning your unconscious for being a rogue thinker and causing all sorts of drama in your life, remember the brilliance of this design. It's a system which allows you to get on with your chosen task at hand, while in the background it keeps everything going, seamlessly, efficiently, and effortlessly, constantly reacting and readjusting to the world around you. That's impressive.

Our unconscious is also registering what we feel about everything: Whether it is the person walking past your desk or the tone of voice used by the waitress serving your coffee, to how you are feeling about the garbage argument. Our unconscious registers through our five senses and then stores all the information just like an enormous database. Most of what it absorbs we don't consciously retrieve but, like it or not, most of the time it is running our show.

THE UNCONSCIOUS PLAYING A MAJOR EXECUTIVE ROLE

It plays a major executive role in our mental lives by collecting, interpreting, and evaluating information. It "can set goals in motion, quickly and efficiently," says Wilson[9]. It is our unconscious that sees the snake before we can consciously process what we have seen and has made us leap out of the way.

One of the compromises of our super speedy unconscious is that it has no power to discern what is truth from what isn't; What is logical versus what is irrational. The unconscious moves fast and takes everything at face value, with no power to weigh it up. It assumes everything is fact, and as you can imagine this can get us into serious trouble.

If your unconscious thinks the boss is talking harshly to you the chances are you will feel resentful and fed up. Deep down this is because the more primitive crocodile part of our brain is signalling danger – we could be threatened. In fact, most of the time when the boss

9   Professor Timothy Wilson, *Strangers to Ourselves: Discovering the Adaptive Unconscious.*

calls you into his office your brain will be on high alert, even if you are not conscious of it. After all he is the larger crocodile on the block and holds more power, which threatens your sense of safety. In to-day's terms we are so aware of our status as a key indicator of how safe we feel.

When we are the boss in a particular situation, perhaps at home organising an event, we feel safer but if our work boss calls us in to criticise or question an aspect of our work, our crocodile brain jumps to the fore. It doesn't matter what position in the organisation you hold, if the boss calls us in we are aware that our 3 'S's could be threatened. However, if you are in the executive suite and your executive assistant comes in to ask you what you need him to do, your brain is relaxed and feels powerful. We are so tuned in to our status, that any perceived undermining will inevitably cause a physical reaction, unless we can control it and talk ourselves down from our heightened awareness.

When we are aware that this is a function of the more primitive part of our brain, we can, if we feel a flutter of anxiety, tell ourselves this is just our crocodile out to protect us. We can identify the feeling, which helps us gain a sense of control, reflect, and engage our neo-cortex, the conscious, rational part of our minds, to analyse what's really going on with the boss. We might see things from a different perspective – for instance, that she is under huge pressure and probably didn't mean to snap at you. This awareness will help us to change our attitude. Our unconscious does not differentiate between what is the truth and what we think is true but may not be. The power of criticism and evaluation is very much part of the conscious mind.

FOOD, SEX, FIGHT OR FLIGHT

In his book, *Getting The Love You Want*, Harville Hendrix[10] describes the unconscious mind well when he says, "The only thing your old

---

10   Dr. Harville Hendrix, *Getting the Love You Want*.

brain seems to care about is whether a particular person is someone to: 1) nurture, 2) be nurtured by, 3) have sex with, 4) run away from, 5) submit to, or 6) attack. Subtleties such as, "this is my neighbour," "my cousin," "my mother," or "my wife" slide right on by. In many ways our unconscious mind is very primitive, hence the nickname, crocodile brain.

Eastern philosophy has long used the metaphor of the unconscious as the elephant and the rider as our conscious will. The rider is trying to control the elephant, which doesn't want to be controlled. When you think that the pre-frontal cortex or neo-cortex takes up just 4% of the volume of our brain, we can see that the unconscious is a vastly bigger and stronger part of our brain, says David Rock in his book, *Your Brain at Work.*[11]

The unconscious is the seat of our memories, our experiences, and everything we have learned. Think of it as similar to your computer – storing everything we have done but incapable of evaluating the validity of the information stored within it. The unconscious's greatest flaw is that it lacks this vital power of criticism and evaluation.

Wilson tells us that the unconscious may be more sensitive to negative information than the conscious self, which can have a huge impact on our fundamental beliefs about ourselves. Most of us grab onto the negative stuff people might say about us and allow the positive to go straight over our heads. This is because the negative is triggering our 3 'S's and as we progress through the 7 keys to empowerment I will talk more about this.

If you are told often enough that you are stupid, then deep down you will believe you are incompetent, and it will take a lot of conscious reprogramming to erase that belief. A teacher may tell you that you are hopeless at math, and forever after you think you are hopeless at math, until you logically think this through and decide that you can do math; after all, you do it every time you look at your bank balance.

11   Dr. David Rock, *Your Brain at Work.*

Imagine as a child you have a fearful mother who is often telling you to be careful. Be careful, you could fall, be careful, what you are doing is dangerous, be careful not to talk to strangers they could be dangerous, be careful of cars, you might get run over, be careful of power points, the electricity could kill you, be careful of water, you might drown.

All of these are typical things we may tell a toddler umpteen times over a number of years in order to keep him safe, and if his Mum is always modelling the same fearful behavior this is what he will learn. It drops into his unconscious, and then it is hardly surprising that the toddler turns into a fearful adult, who has an unconscious belief that the world is not safe.

As a fearful adult it's possible that he will turn out to be very much a 'yes' man, less confident in his own opinion because it could be wrong. This restricts his imagination and creativity, so he is not bringing all of who he is and all of his abilities into his life. He will tend to follow the crowd rather than exert his own personality and style.

OUR UNCONSCIOUS - OFTEN THE ROOT CAUSE OF RELATIONAL PROBLEMS AND SELF-SABOTAGE

An important concept to grasp is that once the unconscious mind has been programmed in a certain way, that will rightly or wrongly, become our truth. And even when we realise the belief is not serving us it takes considerable awareness to break the habit. Some of the unconscious beliefs you hold will be working directly against what you are trying to achieve on a conscious level.

For example: you are busy doing an assignment at work that's out of your normal range of activities and you realise that you are doubting your ability to do it sufficiently well. A little voice in your head keeps saying this will be a failure like all your others and the boss will know that

you are such a failure!

you are not up to it. You have sabotaged yourself before you have really begun.

Or you volunteer to make a cake for a charity cake day and as you start the little voice, that sounds exactly like your mum, starts up saying, you are hopeless at baking, remember that last cake you made that turned out like a slice instead of a cake. Suddenly all enjoyment has gone out of the project and you feel sure it will be a flop. Physiologically that thought has precipitated your brain to send a cascade of cortisol down through your body, which will take seconds to dissipate. This is crocodile brain's way of trying to keep you safe from criticism.

And this is why so many of our relationships and our lives can go wrong without us knowing why or how. Usually we are operating on 'truths' that were laid down when we were children, growing, learning, and reacting to the environment around us. Sometimes those 'truths' and that programming are outdated and irrelevant to our present-day situations, yet we still base our behavior on them.

We have now learned a lot about our brain and you may be thinking this is interesting stuff but how is it relevant? **It is relevant because our brain, particularly our unconscious, drives our relationship behavior and is usually the root cause of most problems and can unknowingly sabotage us.**

It is right here, at this fundamental level, that issues start. The scary thing is that most of us are totally unaware that the crocodile part of our brain is motivating our behavior and causing the problems that all of us encounter in life, or at work at one time or another.

We all like to appear to be in control, but most of the time it's a carefully constructed façade. The trouble is we create it so well that it appears to be, not a disguise, but who we are – and what's more we believe it is who we are. When we become more conscious of the power of our crocodile brain we would be able to be more of the rational person we like to think we are.

CHAPTER RECAP

- There are three wonderfully complex layers within our brain - the conscious, the subconscious, and the unconscious.
- All our behavior is directly motivated by the 3 'S's – survival, safety, and security.
- This comes from our unconscious; whose main purpose is to ensure our survival and keep us safe. When the 3Ss are in place we seek to improve our status.
- Our conscious is the rational thinking part that is essentially logical. We identify with this part of ourselves the most, but we tend to use it the least!
- Our unconscious brain (or crocodile brain) is primal and an exceptionally effective system, which operates outside of our awareness enabling fast and adaptive mental processing of billions of bytes of information.
- The unconscious has no evaluative powers so it perceives situations as the whole truth when in reality it may not be the truth at all.

*This process can be incredibly destructive to our relationships

YOUR JOURNEY

- Can you identify incidents in the past that you now realise was your crocodile brain reacting?
- Can you recall incidents when you exercised strong self-control? (That was your neo-cortex working.)
- Can you think of people in your life that you would like to **imagine** your crocodile brain attacking? If so, now you know you are truly human!
- Can you now imagine your neo-cortex coming into play to control that urge and initiate peace?

CHAPTER 2

The Damage We Do to Ourselves

🔑 THE SECOND KEY

Our instinctive drive to protect ourselves often causes emotional reactivity and destructive patterns of interpersonal interaction.

BUILDING ON WHAT we've learned in the previous chapter about the 3 'S's, our conscious, our subconscious, and our crocodile brain, we now know that our unconscious instinctively interprets situations at lightning speed.

What we will cover in more detail in this chapter is that our parents and caregivers programmed our unconscious as we grew. For the moment it is important to understand that our parents continually modelled all the rules and ways to behave, which dropped into our unconscious to effectively become our blueprint or hard drive.

This programming from early childhood has a direct influence on how we think and behave in our relationships. The next important fact to know is that how we think about something directly influences how we view a situation, whether it is positive or negative.

Let's briefly revisit the neuroscience. To be efficient we know that our crocodile

brain doesn't like to change its mind once it has accepted and programmed in something as a truth. We also like to be right at least 90%
of the time and we are clever at selecting only the information and
evidence that supports our view, while ignoring facts that point in a
different direction.

The science of social psychology teaches us that we will see only
what we want to see, so our psychological immune system works to
keep the world the way we want to see it as well, says Prof Wilson.

The ramifications of this are wide-ranging because we want to
convince others that our opinion is the right one and often the only
correct one! How often have you tried to convince others that you are
right? Certainly, I know I want to be right much of the time!

We often try and persuade others into feeling what we are feeling,
which can lead to the formation of negative cliques. We are unconsciously primed to notice what we may perceive as a conspiring group.
You wonder what they are talking about, and because we are the centre of our own universe we often think they are probably talking about
us. Your 3Ss are aroused and your brain unconsciously engaged.

Or, on a personal front, when we disagree with a spouse or sibling
how often do we go off and try and enlist our friends' support against
the 'bad' other. This tactic is called **triangulation**.

We are not being deliberately manipulative when we try to bring
others in to support our view, we do it unconsciously to try and build
support and solidarity for ourselves. (Again, the 3Ss come into play.)
Most of us don't enjoy being out on a limb; we want to pull others in
to side with us. This is particularly evident in a business environment
where you will often hear the gossip over the coffee machine as we try
and pull our work colleagues into sharing our particular gripe about
someone.

Coming back to wanting to be right, the daunting thing is that the
more often we think something and convince ourselves it is right, the
more truth that thought holds for us and it literally shapes our neural
pathways making physical brain connections.

"Where you focus your attention, you make connections", says neuroscientist Jeffrey Schwartz.[12] Focus your attention on something new, and
you make new connections. This has been shown to be true through studies

---

12   Jeffrey Schwartz, in conversation with Dr. David Rock.

of neuroplasticity, where focused attention plays a critical role in creating physical changes in the brain.

You could think of it as water running down the easiest path. Gradually it wears away a bigger and bigger track. The same with our brain – the more we think a particular thought the more entrenched the neural pathways become in our brain. The more I think I dislike a particular person or situation, the more difficult it becomes to change that way of thinking. It has started to carve a deep pathway in my brain.

The need to be right

One of our major internal battles rages between our need to be accurate and our desire to feel good about our self. How we wage this battle and how it is won are the central determinants of who we are and how we feel about ourselves, says Wilson.

There are major ramifications for us, not only in our personal but also in our business relationships, when we continually think we are right and that the other is lacking. We need to be aware of this very human predisposition because it leads to irrational assumptions and certainly to self-sabotage.

There is a lovely story (probably totally untrue) that clearly illustrates this point:

A battleship and what appears to be another vessel are on a collision course and the captain of the battleship requests the other vessel to change course. The other vessel responds that the battleship should change course and an argument ensues, with the captain of the battleship becoming more heated, and talking of his superior size. Eventually the other 'vessel' says "it's your call, I'm a lighthouse!"

We can clearly see the battleship captain's crocodile brain at play. He did not want to change his mind and was counting on his superior size! We all fall into this trap at one time or another – it starts in kindergarten. For a while we can blame it on our crocodile brain that wants to be right to feel safe and secure, but after we become aware this won't work, if we want to evolve.

We want to make our own decisions and carry out those decisions or be given the autonomy to do what we want to do; because of course we feel we know best. When we have the authority, our crocodile brain feels in control and safer. However, often when we are given autonomy we want the support of others to back us up. This has the added benefit of covering our back and being able to blame others if it all goes wrong. In the business environment we all want autonomy because it gives us a sense of self-importance, status, and control.

Another aspect to consider in our desire to be right is the difficulty most of us have in truly hearing another person without our own subjectivity - emotional and feeling responses getting in the way. Most of the time we don't listen carefully to what another is saying. We sort of assume we know what the other is saying and then are anxious to put our own point of view forward, often not having truly heard what the other person wanted to communicate.

If we focus hard on what the other is saying, we can start to hear all the underlying messages. Addressing these or at least being curious about them takes the focus away from our self and makes our communications flow much more easily. This desire to be right is particularly prevalent at work, largely because we are generally more alert to possible criticism. Our third S, security, could be threatened. Hence at work we will often hear justification and excuses.

A useful exercise is to practise listening. Get someone to tell you something about a problem they are having. After listening carefully, paraphrase what you think they said, and ask them if you understood correctly. It's a shock to think we have listened to someone and then

they tell us we haven't really heard what they have said, or perhaps what has been implied. This happens more often than you would expect. Try using this technique with the people nearest and dearest to you, because they will feel properly heard, and you will get them onside!

REACTIVE BEHAVIOR

When someone disagrees with us or we misunderstand what he or she is saying because of our own unconscious bias, it's easy to get angry and frustrated. This emotion is linked to the crocodile brain's interpretation that we are being threatened. What happens when we feel threatened? Below are just a few examples of behavior that we all probably exhibit at some stage or another, or perhaps feel we have experienced at the hands of another.

- Competition (fear others will be perceived as better than me)
- Lack of cooperation
- Aggressiveness
- Deceit – lying, cheating
- Manipulation
- Withdrawal of recognition and/or lack of recognition
- Frustration at not being fully heard
- Perceived favouritism
- Territorial/empire building as a power base
- Failure to understand the part we play

These are known as positioning strategies, intended - maybe not consciously - to try and get the upper hand. We believe if we get the upper hand we will be safe. Again, this is the crocodile brain in action. (We are seeking to resolve the threat and therefore feel safe.)

If we stop, engage our neo-cortex and think things through, we might see that, while some of these behaviors and strategies may give us a short-term advantage, it will not be in our long-term interest. Most will set us up for a win-lose situation rather than win-win, which ultimately does not achieve the best outcome for ourselves. Remember, crocodiles probably don't think about their long-term future – it is about survival and dominance now.

Jane was concerned that her co-worker Melinda was getting more positive attention from the boss than she felt she deserved. Jane decided it was because Melinda was young and attractive, so she set out to undermine her in any way she could. The company's structure was that new sales information came across Jane's desk first. This made it easy for her to withhold information and try to make Melinda look as if she was out of touch with the latest developments. Eventually Melinda became dispirited with feeling undermined and left. In the short-term Jane had appeared to win.

Surprising though it may seem, we learned all of these positioning strategy behaviors in childhood. We may not have been subtle or sophisticated in how we implemented them, but if you think of the playground I have no doubt you would recognise each and every strategy – each one motivated by our 3Ss.

Often it seems that the same thing is happening now we are adults. We work hard to disguise what we are doing, while it is easy to see the behavior in small children. Almost without fail, these tactics lead to a lack of personal satisfaction in the longer term.

Arguably, the worst thing about this is that our crocodile brain doesn't take any responsibility for our part in fiery interactions. Crocodiles don't like saying sorry; the word doesn't feature in their vocabulary. And remember our unconscious believes that its perspective is 'truth' and therefore it is always someone else's fault. However, the other people involved in the situation, are also at the whim of their crocodile brains and are likely to be acting in a similar way, particularly if they feel threatened.

So here we have a picture of two crocodiles facing each other off. Not a pretty sight, and if one of the crocodiles is more powerful than the other, he/she will generally win the fight and the less powerful one will withdraw, perhaps to fight again later, or try and engage in some strategy to outwit the bigger crocodile.

Deceit, manipulation, undermining, resentment, and sabotage all spring to mind as ways to counteract the bigger crocodile.

CHAPTER RECAP

- Once our crocodile brain has made up its mind, it does not like changing it.
- Our crocodile brain only really wants to see and hear what it wants to see and hear (lighthouse story).
- Neither of which may be fact, nor even reasonably accurate!
- Crocodile brain wants to be right and it wants the autonomy to do what it wants to do.
- We will try and convince others that our opinions are correct in order to shore up a base of support. This forms little cliques. We may do this unconsciously.
- When we feel threatened we can become very reactive in our behavior including aggression, deceit, sabotage, and manipulation.
- We do not want to take any responsibility for the part we play in the interaction; it is usually someone else's fault.
- The other people involved in the fiery interaction or relationship are also at the mercy of their crocodile brain and may be reacting and behaving in the same way you are.

YOUR JOURNEY

- Can you think of times when you were convinced that your proposed course of action was right and should have been followed?
- With the benefit of reflection now, was that the case? Could the other person have been proposing a valid alternative?
- Can you think of occasions when you have been so convinced that you are correct that you did not want to listen to another's perspective?
- Can you think of incidents when someone did not want to listen to you? How did it make you feel; did you take any action and did it impact your ongoing relationship?

CHAPTER 3

Our Brain Still Working on Outdated Software

THE THIRD KEY

Our thinking patterns and behavior today remain largely untouched and unnoticed since programming was laid down in early childhood.

YOUR BRAIN IS like the hardware of an incredibly powerful computer, but you've been operating on software programming that was installed when you were a toddler! Is it time for an upgrade?

This is a frightening thought. Most of us are totally unaware that we work today on understandings and experiences that we absorbed in the first few years of our life. Imagine driving a car today that is 20, 30 or 40 years old. No power steering or power-assisted brakes, no radio, no electric windows, no heating or air conditioning, and the list goes on.

Well, psychologically that is what many of us are doing today – running on value systems laid down into our unconscious by our well-meaning parents or caregivers. And when you think that the programming constitutes 95 – 99% of your processing power it's a chilling thought.

Many of us are working from belief systems that may not even be our own. We are on autopilot reacting from ideas laid down in our unconscious, often before we had even developed any rational powers of critical evaluation, which really is before the age of 5 - 6 years old. At 5 or 6 we are just starting to access our conscious brain. Prior to that we are working totally with our all-powerful unconscious.

In all fairness to our parents and caregivers they were doing the best job they could and they needed to socialise the little crocodile within us, as we, in turn, socialise the little crocodiles we bring into the world. As babies we yelled when we were hungry, wet, or cold and wanted instant attention. Our brain in those very early months of development was just like a little crocodile's. We had to survive and our survival instinct was very strong.

Gradually we developed and grew, our limbic system kicked in, and we realised other people had different preferences to us. We often see 2-4 year olds and older children looking at the new baby in the family and bringing him or her a bottle or a toy. This is the nurturing limbic system at play.

The last part of our brain to switch on was our thinking rational part. Generally speaking, the neo-cortex is slowly coming on line at ages 5 – 6 but is actually not fully developed until the early twenties!

When we are dealing with teenagers, know that their brains are still being wired up. We've all seen toddler tantrums and teenage tantrums! Maybe we remember our own arguments with our parents in those teenage years in which case, we can blame our brain. In very small children the neo-cortex isn't available and therefore they do not have the skill of reason, much to our frustration as adults

TRUTH – OR NOT?

As small children our little brains have so much to absorb. Consequently, everything our parents and our environments tell us is perceived as truth – Father Christmas, magic, and monsters are seemingly real. Our parents had the unenviable task of trying to socialise us and turn us into civilised little people that didn't run amok, taking others' toys, bullying and generally being totally self-absorbed. We were taught the rules of the family and the society we grew up in so that the family and our community could function effectively and efficiently.

All this programming was encoded into our unconscious when we had no evaluative powers to decide its value. Our parental programming formed the blueprint of our lives.

We are generally unaware that this programming is there and underlying all our initial gut reactions. Its power and influence on our everyday actions is enormous.

The relevance of this information about our wonderfully powerful computer brain and early programming is that it can and does harm us without our knowing. Our brain hijacks our best intentions because we only have a very small processor, in comparison with the rest of our brain, to focus on what we want. Unfortunately, as soon as we take our eye off the ball our good intentions go out of the window and we default back to the old programming. Focusing on what we really want requires strenuous effort and repetition to change our programming. More about this to come.

When we understand what is going on under the competent façade people usually present and the more we understand about this fundamental programming the more equipped we will be, not only to know ourselves, but to make more informed choices in our relationships.

NEUROSCIENCE AND EMOTIONS

Let's dive into the neuroscience again

We know that the brain is genetically programmed and develops and matures as a result of ongoing experience. Experience shapes the brain throughout life by altering the neuron connections within the brain. We have literally trillions of neuron connectors and each time we do something new we build more connectors. All mental processes are created by the activity of neurons firing in the brain. Each experience we have raises an emotional response or reaction. Remember the first time you saw the sea or played in snow, went ice skating or dancing. Perhaps your first kiss or sexual experience.

Each of these sensual experiences generated an emotional response, which perhaps you don't remember, but which is nevertheless recorded in your personal database, your unconscious. Their influences will in all probability still be playing out today. You may love or hate the sea, the snow, or dancing and that emotional response will largely stem from those very first experiences, depending on whether they were good or bad. If they were good you probably love the experience.

The emotions we feel in connection with experiences, people, and situations are a fundamental integrating process within the brain and influence our early and ongoing social responses.

> You are at the disco with your friend because she loves to dance. But you hate it; the loud music really puts you off, as do all the people crowded together on a small dance floor, throwing themselves around. You can't think of anything worse and you don't know why you feel as strongly as you do. What your conscious mind doesn't remember, but your unconscious does, is that way back in your past as a toddler you were exposed to a very noisy big family party at Christmas where there was lots of loud music and big people dancing around.
>
> You felt lost in the crowd amongst all the legs and couldn't find your parents. It was a frightening experience for you. That fearful feeling has imprinted itself in your memory and was stored in your unconscious. While you didn't remember the circumstances well it has strongly impacted your current opinion about discos, loud music and feeling trapped in a small space with lots of moving bodies.
>
> Another example: As a small boy you experienced the absolute horror the day Dad came home and said he had lost his job and that there would be no more money coming in. Everything was going to change and the house may have to be sold because your parents would not be able to pay the mortgage. Engraved on your memory at that moment would be the thought that the workplace could be unpredictable and life could change instantly. That response has embedded itself deep into your psyche and whenever there is any office talk of retrenchments you feel your stress level rise dramatically.

EXPERIENCES SHAPE OUR WORLDVIEW

Our experiences influence how we view the world. Each experience generates its own perspective or state of mind that directly impacts our picture of the world and how we respond to each and every circumstance. If most of our early experiences felt safe and we trusted our parents to take good care of us, we will have probably formed an optimistic view of the world and live life accordingly. If, however you were bought up in a war zone and life was dangerous and unpredictable, you would probably have a fearful, untrusting view of the world.

Emotion and social connection go hand-in-hand. When other people feel our emotion, such as feeling happy or sad for us, or we share an emotion, we feel connected, seen or heard. When we feel seen we feel good and our feelings have been met. Of course, the reverse also applies. When we feel unheard, disconnected or alone in our feelings, we feel dissatisfied or sad. These feelings of emotional connection or disconnection are called emotional resonance. What happens in relationships stems from emotional resonance, either positive or negative. It underlies relationships. For example, when we feel slight discomfort in an interaction we instinctively know and feel the emotional resonance is off key.

If it is not quite right, we may not be able to put a finger on exactly why. It is quite likely that the other person is not feeling at ease either and it may be all about them, but you are picking up the energy and that's emotional resonance. Socially it feels uncomfortable.

When both parties feel happy and connected emotional resonance feels right. Again, in the business environment you know immediately what sort of mood your boss is in when you go to ask him/her something. You have read either his emotional openness or his closed mindset and you quickly re-evaluate whether you will go ahead with your request or quietly withdraw to await a more conducive atmosphere.

Let's jump back to the neuroscience again. Although we have a crocodile brain, we also have a limbic system (the caring part) and a neo-cortex (rational, thinking) both newer parts of our brains, which are profoundly relational. We could not survive as a species without being supported by each other. We couldn't live as babies and children without being looked after, so our brains have evolved to be profoundly relational.

FAIRNESS

As humans we are particularly geared to recognising fairness. Remember as children how we were so aware of what was fair and what wasn't. When your brother or sister got something you didn't, you would be the first to notice and complain. Again, these are the older parts of our brain, both crocodile and mammal, coming into play. Our brain evolved to be able to spot who to trust and who was less trustworthy.

This came from being hunter-gatherers. If we killed the bison we couldn't eat it all, with no refrigeration, so would share it out amongst our tribe. This instigated a type of trust system. We had to trust that the person we had given some of our bison to would return the favour when he killed the next bison.

If we found that we didn't receive our fair share we would know not to trust that person next time. We learned the hard way how to identify friend, foe or those who were purely indifferent to our needs. We are good at reading all the signs and fairness is a large signpost for us. Our brain is always checking for fairness.

We have survived and flourished as a species because we can respond readily and accurately to another's intentions. One of the ways the brain does this is by using mirror neurons.

MIRROR NEURONS

Mirror neurons serve to link the emotional expression of one person to another. For example, when we see another person cry we may feel like crying or even cry, although not so likely in a business environment, because we are more aware of keeping our professional mask in place. Likewise, if we see someone angry we may also feel angry. This is why a good movie can be such an emotional roller coaster ride.

Our mirror neurons detect or read another's intention. Mirror neurons, as well as a creative imagination, also may help us to feel how another is feeling and enables us to put ourselves in their shoes, by checking how our own body/mind responds. This is the basis of empathy and compassion. We can instinctively read a situation and can gauge friend or foe.

One implication of this skill is that as small children we will have instinctively gauged our parents' reaction to different situations and this will have dropped down into our unconscious to influence, unbeknown to us, our perceptions of the world.

Being aware of this enables us to quietly question our beliefs to ensure that we are acting out of our own value system and not just parroting old beliefs that may no longer serve us or being walking duplicates of our parents. Reprogramming ourselves, takes constant repetition in order to create new neural pathways to undo our early encoding.

Every time a situation occurs our brain immediately searches our memory banks for a similar experience and the outcome of that initial situation will largely determine our reactions to the current situation. So, without us being aware we are continually dragged back to old pathways usually from many years before. "Issues from our past may influence us in the present and alter how we behave in the future by directly shaping how we perceive what is going on around us and inside us," says Siegel.[13]

This has obvious ramifications for our relationships. We will make some fundamental mistakes if we assume that everyone shares a similar belief system even if we are culturally aligned. Our beliefs are the product of our childhood environment and often do not change unless we consciously look at them and decide if they still serve us and correspond with our current thinking. Our predisposition will be to assume our beliefs are the correct ones and our crocodile brain will find all the reasons to support those beliefs.

---

13   Dr. Daniel Siegel, *The Developing Mind.*

CHAPTER RECAP

- The blueprint of our lives comes from our parental programming.
- This blueprint was encoded when we were extremely young (1-5 years) and before our conscious thinking, evaluative neo-cortex was developed.
- Most of us are still operating on that same programming today and are often unaware of it.
- Our experiences directly influence how we look at the world and how we respond now and in the future.
- Emotion and social connections form a linking process with experience to shape our view of reality, our beliefs, attitudes, and behavior. We are particularly attuned to fairness and trust.
- The emotions we feel dictate how we view the world and direct how we engage with the world around us.

YOUR JOURNEY

- Can you think of times in your life when you became aware of your thinking and decided that you no longer wanted to think a particular way? You recognised that your old thinking no longer served you or was no longer applicable.
- Can you think of incidents when, with additional information, you changed your mind and your perception of someone or something?
- How have experiences that you considered unfair impacted you?

CHAPTER 4

Our Unconscious Influences Us All the Time

🔑 **THE FOURTH KEY**

Programming went into the unconscious and we do not realise that our unconscious influences our every thought and action

What we have learned so far is that our programming and much of our belief system were formed out of conscious awareness, and have been embedded deep into our unconscious mind. Even more frightening is the influence that programming is having on our every thought and action.

We were taught the rules of our family at a very young age, often in very subtle ways. Misbehavior could be noted with the mere raising of an eyebrow, a look or a feeling of being dismissed, not seen, and ignored. Often the messages were the same as our own parents had received as children and passed on with no conscious awareness.

The following example shows how subtle this can all be: you knew you had stepped out of line when Dad raised his eyebrows at you as a child. Raised eyebrows become a trigger for you; they signal danger to our crocodile brain.

Perhaps today your partner or your boss raises her eyebrows when she feels you are lacking in some way or your work is inade-

---

quate. That gesture immediately sends a signal to your brain – be aware, danger is around the corner and you may feel infuriated or insecure without knowing why.

If you are anything like me, my immediate reaction to feeling uncomfortable, is to find fault with the other, either overtly or covertly. In this case we may feel real resentment towards the boss, which then plays out in some way. You could try and pull your co-workers into feeling the same way you do about the boss or you could try and sabotage the boss in some way, undermine her or merely make the atmosphere really uncomfortable.

Back to our programming: parents in an effort to help as well as control their children also try and instil drivers or motivational rules. (Drivers are the phrases that are designed to drive us on.) A few common ones are:

- Don't
- Please others – think of others
- Do as you are told
- Work hard
- Hurry up
- We know best
- You are not worthy
- You do not deserve
- You are always clumsy
- You are rude
- You are not enough
- Be smarter, you are dumb
- Be perfect
- Try harder
- The list is endless and you will no doubt think of lots of your own.
- Try harder

The list is endless and you will no doubt think of lots of your own.

There is a wonderful little 'should' list by famous psychotherapist Virginia Satir who wrote:

"Rules for Being a Good Person

I must always be:

Right

Clean

Bright

Sane

Good

Observant

Healthy

No matter what the cost of the situation

For

Everyone counts more than I

And

Who am I to ask for anything for myself?"

you are such a failure!

I wonder how many of us resonate with some aspect of the above. Can you still remember the frequent criticisms of yourself that you heard as a child and which may still quietly plague you? We talked earlier about how our unconscious may be more sensitive to negative information than our rational, thinking, neo-cortex, our conscious self.

These negative comments usually leave deep scars and often impact on our fundamental beliefs about our self. They are frequently the basis of our self-sabotage because unconsciously we act them out. Negative messages, particularly those received early in life, often act as drivers, which can bring great success in life but sometimes have a high emotional cost. We now know that positive reinforcement is much more productive.

SHAPED BY OTHERS

Our sense of self and our sense of our own identity are defined by our relationships and the way we connect with others, says Siegel.[14] It is shaped both on an emotional and physiological level. Our sense of 'I' is profoundly influenced by how we belong to the group of people around us, the 'we'. We construct the narrative of our lives based on the social context we live in. For example, if people think poorly of us, that is going to have a very detrimental effect on who we think we are and what we believe we are capable of. Conversely if people think highly of us, this is likely to buoy our confidence and our sense of self.

When we are very young our unconscious is particularly attuned to criticism and negativity because it is so vital for us to feel safe and secure. This is why and how our parents and caregivers could, possibly still can, exert so much power. That little look or a comment like: 'I will deal with you later' had real influence. It largely taught us obedience; it was safer to obey the rules. Somehow our survival instinct knew that we would be helpless and unlikely to survive if we displeased our parents too much, so we became conditioned.

NOT ALL BAD NEWS

Before you try to throw off all the social constructs that your parents plugged into your unconscious, remember that … these rules and 'shoulds' are not all bad news. The unconscious and the rules we have absorbed as children largely govern our life, as they are deeply ingrained and are necessary during the first two or three decades of life for biological and social survival. Children do have some discretion as to which parts of their parents' teachings they will accept. While our adaptation was a series of decisions, albeit largely unconscious, they can be undone. We do have the power to change our decisions once they become conscious and in our awareness.

BEING SET UP FOR FAILURE

We can't change what we are unaware of, which is why awareness is important, useful, and enables us to change. It gives us the opportu-

---

14   Dr. Dan Siegel, *The Developing Mind.*

nity to think about and examine the rules and drivers influencing our lives. Even the drivers (those phrases designed to drive us on) such as, work harder, be good, and the multitude of others we heard as children – while seeming innocuous and even helpful at the time – could in fact be setting us up for failure, mainly because it's impossible to always fulfil them. We can't always be everything to everybody and work hard and be perfect. We are human and we make mistakes.

When we fail to live up to these pre-programmed drivers and expectations we castigate ourselves and judge ourselves as failures. Negative self-talk starts and continues its vicious cycle, etching itself ever more deeply into the fabric of our being and physically into our brains. (Self-talk is the mind telling us what to do and think.) It generally keeps up an incessant chatter, which is the only way it knows of fighting to protect us from emotional pain. Unfortunately, its thoughts are often obsessive, repetitive and compulsive, which only adds to our discomfort. (Have a listen right now and hear what your self-talk is saying.) Dr. Tony Grant, Associate Professor of the University of Sydney, calls these 'ANTS' (Automatic Negative Thoughts).

Continually operating under an injunction like 'try harder' sets us up for continual self-criticism. It is important to remind ourselves that it is far healthier and more encouraging to acknowledge what we have achieved, and to give ourselves and others positive reinforcements, than to dwell on what we and others haven't achieved up to now.

Many of these rules may work well for the business you may work for. If we have absorbed the rule that we must work hard, it is likely that we will be in the office early and may be one of the last to leave. If we feel that we are not successful enough we will drive ourselves to work even harder in an attempt to feel more successful and more content.

But while the drivers may work well for business in the short term, they do not necessarily make for a rounded individual who will usually be more creative and well-balanced than a workaholic. If the workaholic doesn't get the recognition he or she feels they deserve, the resentment sets in and they may resort to some less desirable characteristics. Extraordinary as it may seem to us as responsible adults, today we are still driven by what we didn't get as children.

UNCONSCIOUS, UNMET CHILDHOOD NEEDS MOTIVATE OUR BEHAVIOUR

The way we were as children doesn't go away when we grow up. We've looked at how it remains a dynamic part of us through our unconscious programming. What we don't necessarily acknowledge is its power to motivate our current experiences. If we didn't get what we needed as children (and it is worth emphasising that none of us ever had, or could have, the perfect childhood), we continue to seek what we really need through our adult relationships. **Our unmet childhood needs for security and approval continue to haunt all our relationships, until they become conscious.**

We want from our spouses, partners, family, and friends what we didn't get as children. The aspects of our 3Ss that didn't get met continue to plague us. Probably the most common desire we all have is to be thought of as special and worthy. While this is common to virtually everyone (because the crocodile brain thinks it keeps us safe) it is something we seek to hear from others and can motivate much of our behavior. However, it is usually not something we hear often, so we need to say it to ourselves instead.

Paul thinks he is always one step ahead of others, including his boss. As a child, Paul wanted to be good at sports because it seemed excelling at sport was the only way to get his Dad's attention. However, he was more of an academic than a natural sportsman, and his Dad wasn't really interested in his puny sporting efforts.

As a man, Paul married a sporty woman and then was forever trying to keep up with his athletic wife and cope with her frustration that he lagged behind her. As compensation for his frustration and his yearning for recognition he sees himself as better than those around him both socially and at work and is not above claiming others' ideas and putting them forward as his own.

Unfortunately for him his attitude has the unhappy consequence of making him unpopular both with his workmates and his friends, which further aggravates his need for recognition, turning it all into a vicious cycle.

A father never told his daughter that she was his beautiful little princess (I think most women would have liked to have heard that, not sure many of us actually did!) and she married a man who in their courtship told her she was beautiful, but once they were married that all changed.

She craved to be told she was attractive particularly as his sexual interest in her had waned and she had put on weight after the children were born. She was feeling insecure about herself but all her husband said was that I love your insides not your outsides.

This triggered her back to her Dad who said he wasn't going to make her vain by telling her she was pretty; she'd have to earn his love not just be pretty.

Tim has a female boss whom he feels is far too quick to criticise his work which makes his blood boil, as he tries hard to please her. What Tim doesn't realise is that at an unconscious level his boss's criticism reminds him of his somewhat distant, critical, cold mother, who he was always trying to please.

If Tim could consciously become aware of this he could exercise some control over his angry reaction and be more open to taking on board his boss's comments, making for a happier working environment for everyone.

As a child Jane learned to be a 'good' girl and being assertive was dangerous behavior.

Consequently, as an adult Jane is passive and somewhat boring as a friend because she doesn't voice her own opinions, she will say what she thinks others want to hear.

That works for a while, but sooner or later she finds that friends drift away and she doesn't know why.

That is how unconscious ideas, decisions, and desires that we had no idea we had, or were making, rule our lives. To a greater or lesser extent, they dictate our everyday actions and interactions and sabotage our best efforts.

The way to stop this cycle is to become aware and conscious of these patterns. Self-awareness and understanding can free us from the imprisoning inflexible thoughts laid down in childhood. This is where some personal reflection is needed so we can understand why we become emotionally reactive.

CHAPTER RECAP

- As children we were socialised to fit into the family hierarchy.
- We were all taught rules, many of which were unspoken and subtly reinforced.
- We obeyed because it kept us safer and more secure (less threatening for our 3Ss).
- These rules were programmed into our unconscious, absorbed as truth and went unquestioned.
- This laid down a blueprint for how we should behave, what was acceptable, and what was not.
- Most of our behavior today may still be coming from those old injunctions, rules, and drivers. For the most part they are out of our conscious awareness.
- When we start to self-reflect, we can get a handle on those beliefs and their usefulness and decide whether to keep them or update them.
- Unless we become aware, this programming will also underlie all future interactions.
- Unconscious, unmet childhood needs can still motivate our behavior at a very profound level.
- With self-reflection and conscious awareness of why we react the way we do, we have more choice about how we behave.

YOUR JOURNEY

- Spend some time reflecting on what values drive your behavior, particularly when you are under stress, don't get what you want, when there is confrontation etc.
- Are those drivers helpful to you?
- Do they make you feel good about yourself? If not, are they right for you today?
- Can you think of incidents where your drivers have had a negative impact on either you or your relationships?
- What steps will you take to change the drivers that do not work for you?
- What drivers do you choose now as an adult?
- What behaviors will be aligned or consistent with those chosen drivers?

CHAPTER 5

Why We Hide Parts of Ourselves

THE FIFTH KEY

Our programming taught us to hide what was considered unacceptable behavior and it sank into our unconscious (cognitive dissonance).

Probably the first question you ask is what on earth is cognitive dissonance? It is a psychological concept that in the simplest terms means we don't want to know about something if it's too uncomfortable. It is the discomfort we feel when we find ourselves doing things that don't fit with what we know to be right. For example, we know we should credit the person that came up with the great idea, yet we don't want to lose the kudos it has brought. While we feel uncomfortable stealing someone's idea we do it anyway and feel somewhat awkward.

Another example: we know we should not steal and we try very hard to be honest, but we might try to diddle someone or not correct a mistake that works in our favour. We try hard to reduce the discomfort we feel around those decisions.

A personal example that really bought this concept home to me happened when my baby son Max was sitting in the supermarket trolley. As I unloaded the groceries into the car the trolley got lighter, rolled away, and then flipped over. Max fell out and started crying with a bleeding mouth.

I felt awful – why didn't I foresee what would happen. I scooped him up and took him home. Later when my husband came home I told him what had happened and he looked at Max and said the accident had pushed his tooth back into the gum. I could not believe it but one of his two first baby teeth had been pushed back inside his gum. I wanted to deny that the tooth had ever come through, and difficult though it may be to believe, I genuinely believed that the tooth had never come through. For me this was a classic case of cognitive dissonance.

In fact, it heralded a turning point in my life and was the start of my psychological studies. I could not believe that I had honestly thought that the tooth had not come through. It was only because I trusted my husband completely that I could start to look at what had happened and marvel at how my brain desperately wanted to present another story.

You may be thinking: why do I need to know all this material? What I want are the keys to better relationships to improve my life, not a treatise on my childhood programming. Yet the most important and difficult fact to grasp is that who you are today all started in childhood, and everything about us stems back to childhood, and always will unless we do this work of understanding.

The fact is your essence was built in those early days and what happened in your childhood substantially impacts your relationships today. We are focusing on it here so that you can understand yourself better.

When we can understand ourselves better all our relationships flow more easily. When we have a clearer appreciation of who we are and where we came from we will also understand others more easily. The payoff of this work is that it makes managing others much easier, particularly if interactions start to spiral out of control.

Every time we feel an extreme or intense emotion such as being very angry, frustrated, intolerant or wanting to plot revenge, our crocodile brain is in charge. It's a sobering thought if we think of all the times in the day when we can feel so out of sorts with another.

What a delight if we could choose to engage our rational thinking brain rather than reacting emotively from the crocodile brain. It would certainly give us the power or upper hand when things become volatile.

In chapter 2, we talked about how once the unconscious has made up its mind about something it doesn't want to change and looks to find any evidence and justification to support its world view, while quietly ignoring any facts that may contradict it. This is what we are going to explore in depth with this fifth key understanding.

OUR EARLY SELF HOLDS THE KEY
TO OUR CURRENT SELF

Let's briefly recap what we know about our earliest self.

We know that when we were born our unconscious ruled. It is the oldest part of our brain (crocodile brain) and its main purpose was, and is, to ensure we survive.

Little crocodiles are not particularly social, so we had to be socialised by our parents to ensure that society survived and did not turn to anarchy, which it would have if we hadn't all been socialised. Our instinctive desire as little crocodiles was to take what we wanted, when we wanted it, with no thought of anyone else. When we couldn't get what we wanted we manipulated, schemed, bullied, and fought. Remember all we were concerned with was survival and getting our 3Ss satisfied. Being part of a family, however, it was vital that we were socialised; We were taught the family rules.

Some rules were overt but many were covert. Little by little we were programmed with many behaviors, values, and ideas. That programming formed our blueprint, one full of beliefs and drivers that are probably not even ours, if we stopped long enough to examine them. All those rules, injunctions, and beliefs were imprinted before our brain was developed enough to be able to differentiate between those that we may agree with and those we don't.

SOCIALISATION

With that in mind, let's move to the fifth key.

During our socialisation process we came to understand that it was wrong to steal, to bully, to fight, and all those other 'bad' things we were told we were doing. We learned quickly how to be 'good' children because otherwise our 3Ss were threatened and we did not feel safe or loved.

We know from our brain structure that we are hardwired to be profoundly relational; we thrive when we work together. The fear of not getting the attention and love from our parents or caregivers was very strong. All this made us much more susceptible to being moulded into a socially acceptable shape.

However, our basic instincts did not magically disappear because our crocodile brain is our brain's foundation. We did not suddenly turn into perfect little cherubs, and being smart, we learned to adapt. We learned to hide the 'naughty' parts of ourselves so we would still get the love and attention we needed. We learned that if we didn't behave and hide the 'bad' parts we would usually get punished. That threatened our core need for survival.

The result of all this was that we became 'adapted' (nicely programmed) children. Our free crocodile child was educated to fit into the system. We learned to obey the rules to a greater or lesser extent. We accepted that others knew best.

Consequently, and here is the sad, disappointing part, we absorbed the idea that there were parts of us that were bad or unacceptable. Those parts didn't just magically disappear. Either they were suppressed and went underground, into our unconscious, stored away only to come out when we thought others were not watching; or maybe cognitive dissonance enabled us to forget we even had 'bad' parts at all.

OUR SECRET SELF

The sad thing about being civilised is that, although it is probably "humankind's greatest achievement, it culls out the characteristics that are dangerous to the smooth functioning of our ideals. Anyone who does not go through this process remains a 'primitive' and can have no place in a civilised society. We are all born whole, but somehow the culture demands that we live out only part of our nature and refuse other parts of our inheritance."[15]

We have all suppressed things we don't like about ourselves or think are unacceptable. We even go as far as disguising it from ourselves – for example: I don't want to share my chocolate, but I don't want to acknowledge to myself that I'm mean or that I want the largest slice of pie; I don't return the extra money the shop assistant gave me when she gave me too much change, but I'm not going to recognize that it could be looked on as taking advantage of another; I lie about the amount of alcohol I have drunk when the police stop me on the road; I tell my boss I am sick when really I am just tired and want a day off; I lie when my girlfriend asks me if she looks fat in her dress; I deceive when I say the cheque must have got lost in the post because I definitely sent it when a bill is outstanding. And the list goes on. We have all done it. It may flash through our mind that our behavior is not the best, but we justify it to ourselves saying everyone does it.

All of these hidden traits, that are instinctively part of human nature, get suppressed down in our unconscious. Perhaps at some point they helped our survival as a species, but they are now generally considered socially unacceptable.

I have called all our 'bad' parts our 'secret self', which as we now know is buried in our unconscious. (One of the founders of modern psychology, famous psychiatrist Carl Jung, called this the shadow, but for ease of understanding I called it the secret self.)

---

15   Dr. Robert A. Johnson, *Owning your own shadow.*

46 | YOUR BRAIN: FRIEND & FOE

In effect we disown our secret self as in the examples above. This learning to disown our secret self started, as young children, because back then there was so much information we had to absorb that we couldn't or didn't have the physical ability to deal with difficult or painful information.

It takes energy, time, and sophisticated thought processes to self-reflect on our behavior, which as kids we didn't have the resources to do. Now as adults, it still takes a lot of time and energy to think through our behavior carefully and most of us don't bother.

However, it also takes a lot of energy to keep our secret self-hidden or suppressed, to present the 'perfect' façade. Our secret self "often has an energy potential nearly as great as that of our ego," says noted author and Jungian analyst, Robert Johnson. [16]

Mrs. Perfect keeps a perfect house and garden, everything is immaculate and Mrs. Perfect is also a pillar of society, working voluntarily for charity, as well as generally being very helpful to others. She appears just perfect. There is one little hiccup in her life and that is her neighbour Mrs. Untidy, who as her name suggests is very messy. Her house and garden are an eyesore.

Unfortunately, Mrs. Perfect's kitchen and family room look over Mrs. Untidy's garden which is strewn with an old car wreck, furniture and general junk. It drives Mrs. Perfect mad. She has reported it to the council as a health hazard but to no avail. Eventually Mrs. Perfect decides to take matters into her own hands and one-day sets fire to Mrs. Untidy's house. Eventually her crime is discovered and she is sent to jail. All Mrs. Perfect's hard work in establishing herself as a pillar of society comes unstuck. Her secret self has emerged and caused havoc.

Let's look at how this happened. As a child Mrs. Perfect learned that to be safe she needed everything to be perfect. She got into trouble from her Mum if her bedroom was messy so she suppressed her natural carefree messy child self, it went into her secret, disowned self and she focused her attention on being as perfect as she could be.

---

16   Dr. Robert A. Johnson, *Owning your own shadow.*

Despite this there was a part of Mrs. Perfect, as there probably is in all of us, that couldn't care and would be quite happy to live in total mess with no responsibility for a while. Problem is that Mrs. Perfect could never acknowledge that to herself, it was deeply hidden but she felt that Mrs. Untidy's mess reflected badly on her and at an unconscious level she felt unsafe. (Remember her childhood programming was to keep everything tidy otherwise there could be big trouble.)

When we don't acknowledge our less pleasant but very human characteristics, our secret self will come out to play and does so as soon as our guard is down.

WHEN HIDDEN TRAITS EMERGE
UNINTENTIONALLY AND CAUSE CHAOS

How often have we seen high profile people, who have worked really hard to get to those heights by being model members of society, come crashing down because they have lied about their behavior?

If we look at some of the well-known US politicians such as Bill Clinton, Eliot Spitzer (former governor of New York), and recently Anthony Weiner, they were brought undone by trying to hide their humanness under a cloak of perfection.

In the above cases their secret self-emerged, as it did with the great cyclist Lance Armstrong and his continual denial of the use of performance enhancing drugs until he was eventually exposed. Martha

Stewart, a household name in the US, was brought undone by insider trading. History is littered with people who have fallen short of the expectations they have worked so hard to build.

Secretly we probably all want to be thought of as close to perfect as possible and have the accompanying façade; however, we are all human and inevitably fallible.

So why do we strive for perfection? Again, this is our unconscious and programming coming into play – if we are exceptional we think we are safe and often work extremely hard to be thought of as wonderful. However, as in the cases above, their secret selves eventually emerged to leave a trail of destruction pain and chaos. When we don't acknowledge our less pleasant but very human characteristics, our secret self will come out to play and does so as soon as our guard is down.

We are now getting to the cutting edge of why relationships go wrong.

Operating at an unconscious level we find others to carry the energy of our disowned, suppressed parts. This sounds extraordinary, but this is what we do. And what makes it even more extraordinary is that it happens out of our conscious awareness. We call this phenomenon projection. When we become aware of projection it is easy to spot.

THE START OF PROJECTION

Here's a quick example of projection which we will cover in more detail in the next chapter:

Joe is jealous of Adam's new car but doesn't want to admit this. He has been conditioned to believe that jealousy isn't a nice trait, so he says to Adam, "how wonderful, you are lucky and you deserve it, I'd love a car like that".

Sounds friendly on the surface and Joe is partially genuine when he says it, yet every time he looks at the car he feels angry muttering under his breath: "can't think why he gets a car like that while I am so much better at my job than him. I should be getting paid more so I can get a car like that."

What's happening? Joe may be pleased for Adam at some level but he is envious and his self-talk puts Adam down. Joe is feeling resentment that he is not getting paid more. Beneath the surface bitterness is starting to grow, which in due course could contaminate the relationship between the two men.

If Joe had been more aware, he would have owned his jealousy and acknowledged it, instead of denigrating Adam. We all feel envy or have felt it at some stage and that's normal. The pitfall or trap is what we do about the feeling.

If we take a minute to face what is making us feel angry, upset or irritated, we can acknowledge it and then decide whether it is helpful or unhelpful. We don't need to find fault with the innocent party who has a fancy car or end up resenting our boss or our jobs because we want to be paid more.

Joe has **projected his discomfort** onto Adam and his boss, and disguises this by believing he is a victim, life is unfair. Focusing on Adam and his boss stops him being pro-active and keeps him stuck in the past.

Miranda hates people who cheat the system. Her programming and belief are that cheating is very wrong so she is very attuned to spotting people who can rort a scheme and generally will report them. She told company authorities when a co-worker claimed expenses he had not actually made.

She prides herself on being scrupulously honest. However recently she attended a workshop where at the end of the two days there was a celebratory dinner to which partners were invited and their dinner had to be paid for by an honesty system. Miranda brought her partner to the dinner yet forgot to pay for him!

To recognise behavior and other people's emotions we need to have felt them to some degree ourselves. To recognise murder does not mean that you are a murderer and can kill people; however, chances are you will have killed a mosquito landing on you or a spider or a cockroach in your cupboard. So, while you are not a murderer you can kill.

What we see in others will always be there to some degree in ourselves. If you spot it, you've got it or at least degrees of it. And that is OK. It all goes wrong when we don't admit it. Miranda was acting as a policewoman, reporting her co-worker and being scandalised that he could be dishonest; yet she was being dishonest herself in not paying for her partner at the dinner, just sneaking him in.

The scale of the offence may be different but not what underlies her action. Miranda was projecting her own disowned ability of 'cheating and being dishonest' onto her co-worker. She then covered it from herself by her righteous indignation because she could not accept that she also had the ability to be dishonest. Yet, she too cheated the system. To give Miranda her due, she was no doubt totally unaware of what she was doing.

Can you see how people project? The first step is to suppress the traits that society deems unacceptable. They drop into our unconscious, out of conscious awareness, but these traits don't disappear, they are just hidden. In order to hide them or their urges, we are much more likely to point them out in other people and thus take the heat off ourselves.

If others consider Miranda honest and righteous, they would never suspect her of being a cheat herself. She would no doubt have a hundred excuses as to why she rorted the system by not paying for her partner. The trap is that in justifying her behavior to herself, she avoids having to admit that she too has the ability to cheat and be dishonest.

CHAPTER RECAP

- Our childhood programming taught us that there were many parts of ourselves that were unacceptable – the lying, cheating, bullying, aggressive parts – and in order to be loved and get the attention we needed they had to be suppressed and hidden away.
- We were socialised. These disowned parts didn't just go away as they are fundamental to our crocodile brain and underlie all our human characteristics. They also helped us to survive.
- Collectively, these behaviors, traits, and characteristics, became our 'Secret Self'.
- It takes energy to cover these disowned aspects of ourselves so we find another to carry the aspects of our self that we don't think are acceptable. This is called projection.
- When you spot another's flaws, know that you've got that same flaw or at least degrees of it.
- If you are aware of this very human behavior, can admit it and accept it – you will have a choice about using projection, which is empowering.

YOUR JOURNEY

- Think of someone you really dislike, what are the particular characteristics you detest?
- Can you acknowledge aspects of yourself that might have some similarity to those you dislike?

CHAPTER 6

Focusing on Other's Faults

🗝️ **THE SIXTH KEY**

To avoid looking at our own imperfect characteristics we focus on others' faults – PROJECTION

This is where all the psychological underpinning starts to come together and the work gets more difficult. It takes courage to take this well-known psychological principle on board and to admit that you project. Let's be really clear about this – we all project and we project 24/7.

I see the world through the lens of my experience.

Yes and if you and I were running it, everyone would think like us and it would be great.

We project because we view the world through our own lenses, which have been built up of our own experiences, expectations, and beliefs. We can't really see or do things differently unless we do this work.

If you choose to read on, you will be stepping through the Looking Glass as in Alice in Wonderland and there is no stepping back. Once you understand the principle, it brings awareness and eventually responsibility. While we are unaware we just keep going our merry way projecting here, there, and everywhere, seeing all the faults in others that we don't believe we have or are even capable of having.

As they say, ignorance is bliss. The downside of that ignorance is that our relationships suffer and often cause us considerable grief. We spend a lot of time sabotaging ourselves without even realising it.

Before we dive into the mechanics of projection, it is important to realise that it stems from an unconscious need that we all share. At a deep level we all want to be loved, cherished, validated, and thought to be wonderful! We would also like to be looked after 24/7, as long as that does not interfere with whatever we want to do.

Imagine a perfect person who did everything you wanted, who took complete care of you, with none of the downside of having to think of what their needs might be, sort of like an intelligent loving slave! The bad news is that this scenario is completely idealistic.

However, that does not prevent us striving to get it and, worse still, continuing to look for it even though our thinking rational neo-cortex knows better. This very basic underlying human need to be loved, cherished, and be in relationships with perfect others, contaminates all our interactions to some degree unless we can be realistic.

THE IDEAL PARENT

For a moment let's imagine we are children and look at what we want from the ideal parent:

- Loves us unconditionally
- Overlooks our faults
- Even better, doesn't see any faults
- Is not harsh with us
- Agrees with what we want
- Praises us often
- Is fair

Anyone disagree with that?

THE IDEAL CHILD

Now let's imagine we are parents. What would we want from the ideal child?

- Always obedient
- Always loving
- Always achieves
- Enhances our reputation as a parent in every way!

Wow, wouldn't that make parenting a breeze?

THE IDEAL PARTNER

- Would your ideal partner look something like this?
- Loves me passionately and says he/she always will
- Says I'm the most important thing in the world to him/her
- Compliments me about my looks, body, personality, intelligence, sex appeal, charm, and everything else about me
- Is willing to drop everything to do whatever I want
- Is prepared to put my needs above his/hers
- Amuses me, entertains me, and gives me space when I need it

Wouldn't that be perfect? Could perhaps eventually get a trifle dull

THE IDEAL EMPLOYEE

Let's look at the ideal employee:

- Is always enthusiastic and prepared to do any extra work that may be necessary
- Is intelligent
- Takes initiative and comes up with good ideas
- Is careful and doesn't stuff up

- Is responsible
- Is always of a cheerful, happy disposition
- Doesn't spend any time on personal matters
- Is loyal and doesn't gossip with other employees
- Makes me look good as a boss
- Is good value for what I pay

Perfect if I'm the boss …

THE IDEAL BOSS

How about the ideal boss?
- He/she is very understanding and kind
- Understands that I have a life outside work
- Wants me to do interesting, stimulating work, not boring, repetitive old stuff
- Wants to give me responsibility when I want it, but is prepared to take the rap if I stuff up
- Wants me to take initiative and have autonomy, but again will take responsibility if it doesn't work out
- Rewards me in many different ways: money, praise, time off, good trips etc.
- Is always fair

Nice …

Wouldn't life be just perfect if others could provide the above? However, unless we can be all of the above to everybody 24/7, we are just plain dreaming! And that is the sad reality of it. So now, knowing that we are not all perfect, let's look at what we do when life doesn't give us the above.

THE OLDEST TRICK IN THE BOOK

We project. Projection is the tool we use to identify those traits in others that we do not want to see in ourselves. Projection comes from a deep, largely unconscious level of fear that if people see our displeasing traits they will not like us and at some level reject us. (3Ss not being met.)

Projection is constantly flashing signposts at us. We will know it is either occurring or ready to occur when we feel strongly about someone, or more particularly when we actively dislike a particular characteristic someone is displaying. Perhaps when you feel reactive about the following behaviors: lying, manipulation, arrogance, bullying, coercing, blaming, criticising, laziness, conceit, dictatorial attitudes, cunning, sabotaging, lustiness, and the list goes on and on, projection may be coming into play.

For example, the adulterous wife accuses her husband of having an affair. The lazy husband accuses his wife of being indolent. The bully accuses another of harassment. A pacifist says he could never kill and then gets the insecticide to destroy the spider.

Just think for a moment about the attributes you hate the most. This intense dislike of particular traits usually signposts your own predisposition towards them. The greater the emotional response to a trait the more resonance it has with us personally. In an ideal world all emotions are quite neutral. What I mean about the neutrality of an emotion is that it assumes a quality of 'just is'.

Let's look at arrogance. Is there someone in your life who you believe thinks she is better than you? She often seems to have an air of superiority. Recognise the characteristic?

What's the opposite of arrogance? Perhaps humility, modesty, and self-diffidence. Someone who doesn't put on airs and graces and is humble and certainly doesn't big-note herself.

If we put these characteristics on a continuum, or a sliding scale, they would probably look like:

Subservient → Humility

or

Unassumingly Confident → Arrogance

Ideally, we would find ourselves in the middle of the continuum, just quietly confident in our abilities. At times we can feel humble in the face of brilliance or great creativity; and in different circumstances sometimes we may feel superior - more intelligent or wiser - than another and move towards the arrogant end of the spectrum. If we are more aware of arrogance than humility, that is a signpost for us that at times we possibly err on the arrogant side.

Most of us secretly, or not so secretly, want to be better than the next person because that's our crocodile brain at play, wanting to be safe. Most of the time our judgement is out in full force and we genuinely think we are better than others, perhaps we are. This is another trip up point for us that can be instrumental in our own self-sabotage.

On the personal front let's look at love, which has so many different shades. It can be tempestuous like passionate romantic love, or deep and quiet like you may have for your grandmother. If we put love on a continuum as below:

Indifference → Love → Grand Passion

We see indifference on one end of the spectrum and grand passion on the other. Our feelings move along the continuum. For instance, grand passion will slowly fade back towards the middle as no one can sustain the demands of grand passion for very long. (Grand passion is expecting our every need to be met by another. Unfortunately, it does not last as we slowly realise our great love has his or her own faults, needs, and desires and can't give us everything we want all the time – not to mention the energetic cost of grand passion.)

Of course, there are different levels of love but when it feels comfortable and easy our emotional response is relaxed. When the emotional response is relaxed it is not signalling projection.

Hate is a different cup of tea:

Love → Indifference → Hate

Hate generates significant energy; there is nothing quiet or passive about it. It is not a relaxed emotional response that 'just is.' It does not sit in the middle of an emotional continuum. When we feel strong emotions like hate we are looking at some level of projection.

When we use substantial energy to deny some trait, behavior or characteristic, know that projection is present. We need to recognise that what we are seeing in others we are capable of. It is part of our secret self that is alive and flourishing. As famous spiritual teacher and author Eckhart Tolle says:

***

"Anything that you resent and strongly react to in another is also in you".[17]

---

17   Eckhart Tolle, *A New Earth: Awakening to your life's purpose.*

Samantha is very dissatisfied with her de facto relationship with Will. She complains that when they do the household groceries she always pays the bill. Will conveniently forgets his credit card, or doesn't have any money, but says he will pay next time. Samantha is very careful with her money and does not like spending it. To her, money represents security and when she supports Will her nest egg is depleted. She feels resentful particularly as in her mind the relationship goes all Will's way. When Samantha challenges Will he says, "It doesn't really matter because we are a couple. Everything I have I want to share with you anyway." This keeps Samantha hooked into the partnership until she tires of empty promises and decides to leave Will.

In the past, Samantha had been stung by criticisms of meanness and stinginess from her family and some friends, which had hurt. Rather than focus on whether she was being mean she could avoid her discomfort by focusing on Will's lack of financial contribution. Projecting meanness onto Will, allowed her to feel better about herself. Like Samantha, unconsciously we tend to pass that hurt on by concentrating on someone else's mistakes and undoubtedly Samantha had a valid point; Will was avoiding his responsibilities.

This story has a happy ending, when Samantha understood what was really going on she was able to talk about it with Will. They laughed about their similarities, and the relationship strengthened. The money issue had to be identified and separated for Samantha to appreciate how it had contaminated her whole perspective of the relationship. When she could identify why and how her mean trait had developed she was able to accept this trait within herself, it was no longer disowned. At that point she also realized she had a choice. She chose not to sabotage the relationship by talking about it with Will. This enabled him to see the part he had unwittingly played and he realized that if he wanted the relationship he had choices to make around responsibility.

A general rule of thumb to understand projection is: 'if you spot it you've probably got it' or at least tendencies towards it. We are all in exactly the same boat; we have faults and we are able to see the faults in others. It is fine to see that someone is lying or cheating as long as we have the awareness to know that there have been times when we too have lied or cheated. Someone who is law-abiding will notice people who break the law and will be quick to judge them. Remember how quick Mrs. Perfect was to judge Mrs. Untidy. Our secret self - all those traits that we disown in ourselves - jump out when we can see them in another and we love to point out their flaws. It makes us feel better and helps us keep our perfect façade intact, or so we think.

> *Malcolm was quick to find fault with Anne, particularly her lack of attention to detail, which he felt was sloppiness. He used any opportunity to point out her flaws to whoever would listen, from the receptionist, her direct reports, to her manager.*
>
> *Anne was on the same management level as Malcolm and he saw her as competition, so consciously felt threatened and was trying to undermine her.*
>
> *While others could see what he was doing, Malcolm was unaware that his behavior was being noted and working against him. In fact, the sloppiness he was busy pointing out in Anne was being reflected in his own work because he was so busy monitoring Anne.*

Projection is the oldest trick in the book and has been part of mankind's armoury since we first walked on the earth. Jesus made one famous comment about projection when he said, "Cast out the log in your own eye, so that you can see the mote in your brother's eye" (Matthew 7:5 and Luke 6:42 - The Bible). Awareness of our projections, like the secret self, is a portal into part of our unconscious. It is important to understand it well, because it plays a huge role, not only in all our relationships, but also in understanding why we self-sabotage as we will see in the seventh and last key to understanding.

PROJECTION IS NOT ALL BAD

Projection is not all bad and negative. We project onto people we admire. We may envy some of their characteristics without realising that we have similar characteristics. When we recognise creative genius in another, know that we have a degree of that wonderful characteristic, – an amazing thought. The traits may not be as well-developed but nevertheless they are there, otherwise how would we recognise them?

When we admire courage, strength, intelligence, grace or charm, appreciate that by identifying these traits in others we have the same attributes to some extent and can embrace and celebrate them as part of us.

Projection also serves a valuable purpose as a protective, defensive coping mechanism. It takes the aspects of our secret self that we cannot accept and sees them in others. The more we lack insight and

awareness into our own behavioral characteristics the more we will project. It allows us to cope when we are not ready to confront our own traits, (perhaps as a first step to embracing them).

Becoming aware of our strong emotions and setting aside some time to reflect is a big step forward. We may not have the resources, time, and courage to deal completely with every situation, so projection lets us set aside certain issues for the time being while signposting the situation.

Let's look at the following example. Alan has been asked to give a quote for an IT service for a large chain of departmental stores. He has underestimated the complexity of the quote and rushing to finish it in time he realises that some key elements have been forgotten which will dramatically impact the costing.

As Alan is realising this he is immediately taken back to the last time he rushed a quote and the job was accepted; however, Alan lost money on the project. In this instance, as he thinks about the current quote, he is projecting his frustration and anxiety from the last situation on this current quote and feels a sense of foreboding. But that was then and Alan is in a different situation now, particularly if he gives himself a moment to think about what is going on emotionally.

Anxiety is starting to overwhelm him and the feeling of being late on the quote sends him into a tailspin. If Alan could have stopped and thought objectively about what signals his anxiety was sending he could have prevented the tailspin. From the neuroscience perspective once in the tailspin his neo-cortex was starting to shut down and rational thinking was going out of the window.

OUR BODIES SEND US SIGNALS

Our bodies send us vital signals. When there is emotional heat or reactivity our body is waving a red flag at us, such as in the example above. Or sometimes we get hold of an idea and go around and around with it, particularly if we think we are right and the other is wrong. Remember how our crocodile brain wants to be right. The trick is to tear ourselves away from our own moralistic soapbox long enough to observe ourselves objectively.

Personally, I find that my moralistic soapbox is a comfortable place to be. I go around and around, like a dog with a bone, justifying my actions to myself. Emotions and physical reactions give us the opportunity to reflect and signal a valuable insight coming from our crocodile brain. I call these emotional signals triggers.

They will usually prompt a bodily reaction, i.e. anxiety or discomfort.

We may focus on our anxiety about something or a particular situation, and avoid looking at what purpose our anxiety is serving, what underlies our anxiety.

The same applies when we are feeling uncomfortable. To avoid doing the detective work of investigating what is going on at a deeper level, we will come up with diversionary tactics such as keeping ourselves extremely busy so there is no time for self-reflection.

We may engage in addictive behavior such as alcohol, drugs, gambling, sex, sport, and the list goes on. We may divert our attention by diving into work, looking at social media, turning on the television, talking to our friends about what is going on for them, eat, immerse ourselves in the computer or with a book.

Our diversionary distracting tactics are endless. I compulsively clean when I am feeling uncomfortable. We are extremely skilled at avoiding looking at what is behind our own emotional states.

What you resist persists

You've probably heard the expression, what you resist persists. This is because everything in our world is built around a dynamic tension between opposing forces. There is a balance between rest and activity, expansion and contraction, summer and winter, night and day, and so on.

When you think of your uncomfortable feelings, or your difficult relationships, you create a dynamic tension by wanting them to improve or change. Wanting something implies that you do not already have it, so we create tension. For example, you have some money yet you want more. The focus is not on the money you have but on what you do not have. While you continue to think about what you do not have you make it a bigger issue. It becomes all about what you do not have rather than what you do have.

What you resist persists, because you continue to ruminate about it. You actively try to achieve something and by giving it more and more of your attention you fuel the issue and it gets worse. One solution is to focus on what you want to achieve with the money; what you want to use it for, the car, the holiday or the house etc. This shifts the focus to being pro-active rather than a victim of circumstance.

In the case of a relationship, try to focus on the aspects that do work and not the ones that don't work. Perhaps try and focus on what you would like to see, instead of all the bad and unsatisfying aspects.

The trick with relationships is to isolate the particular characteristic or characteristics you are finding difficult about the other person, then go back through your memory banks and see if you can find the earliest example of those same characteristics irritating or causing you anxiety or distress.

It may be way back in childhood or at school or it may be a more recent situation. It is highly likely that the crocodile part of your brain, remembering the earlier situation, is signaling danger and is projecting the outcome of that earlier incident onto what is happening now in the current difficult relationship.

Thinking about your own relationships, rather than focusing on all the negatives, imagine how it looks as a successful joyful connection and keep your focus on the positive, on all that does work well. This takes discipline as it is easier for our brain to focus on the negative. Steve Jobs wouldn't have built Apple if all he saw were the obstacles ahead of him. The same would apply to Richard Branson. No great sportsman or woman gets to the top without the initial dream and then the persistent focus. Tolle says: "acknowledging the good you already have in your life is the foundation for all abundance".[18]

POLARITIES ARE NEUTRAL

These polarities are the driving force of all action. They are neither good nor bad; they just are. However, by creating the polarity, for instance in wanting discomfort to go away, you are actually creating a tension that enables you to feel the discomfort more intensely. If you can allow the discomfort to be there, to sit in it, it will subside.

For most of us the need to avoid unpleasant feelings is so strong that to stay within the discomfort may seem a strange idea. In today's world we want and expect instant gratification and resolution. However, if we stay with the tension and

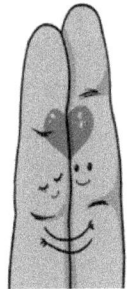

---

tolerate those moments of chaos and confusion, we can generally find a more profound and lasting solution.

When we are feeling discomfort we usually fish around for someone or something to project onto as that allows us not to feel our discomfort so acutely. Instead of avoiding feeling discomfort and projecting onto others, it is healthier to allow the feeling to be there, think about it, accept that it is how you feel right at this moment, and then allow it to pass.

Acknowledging the feeling enables it to pass more easily. It's as if it has been heard. It becomes unhealthy when we can't stop ourselves thinking about a particular negative emotion and it becomes an obsessive loop. I know that one well.

When we sit in our feelings and accept them it: a) gives us the space to accept ourselves and forgive ourselves, and b) gives us the opportunity to gain perspective and choose our actions carefully rather than have knee-jerk reactions to rid ourselves of discomfort. Sitting with the feeling, in ambiguity, can allow different perspectives to open up.

Ian was fed up with his home situation. He was feeling nagged by his wife, feeling he has to be at her beck and call, especially during the weekends. As he stayed with his anger and frustration instead of getting mad with his wife, it occurred to him that his wife demanding his attention was perhaps her way of wanting him close at weekends.

He was surprised at this thought and talked to his wife to try and confirm if this was correct. When she affirmed this for him he felt differently and agreed to do things together for some of the time but said that he also needed to have his own time. Their marital situation improved dramatically. If only all partnership dynamics could be so easily solved!

WHAT WE FACE DISSIPATES

You can add to the phrase, 'what we resist persists' with 'what we face dissipates.' Our fears arise from what we do not confront, not from what we examine. When we look fully and deeply at the source of the discomfort and the fear driving it, the fear loses some of its intensity and power. The truth is that there is nothing within us that can hurt us.

After all, whatever is inside us is what we have already felt and judged. It is our fear of the pain of re-experiencing our own feelings that keeps us trapped. This is an important point and bears repeating: The truth is that there is nothing within us that can hurt us. What is inside us is what we have already felt and judged. It is our fear of re-experiencing our own pain and feelings that keeps us trapped.

> *Duncan was retrenched. This was terrifying as he had accumulated huge debts due to his drug problem and his landlord had given him notice for late rent payments. Without a job he was in a dire situation with no one to fall back on for help and nowhere to live.*
>
> *He had to live on the street until he found work again. Eventually he found work and painstakingly rebuilt his life. However, he was so ashamed of that period of his life that he shut it away and never talked about it.*
>
> *When he was able to acknowledge his earlier irresponsible behavior and talk about it, he realised that he had learned an invaluable lesson and instead of shutting that period away he used it as an illustration of what can happen to help and inspire others. The energy he used to keep it hidden was now liberated and he felt clearer and better about his life.*

Often, we will say, "I don't want to think about that again, it's over and forgotten." Yet when we face our fears and the situations that we dislike we don't necessarily find immediate resolution, but if we can be courageous enough to sit within the tension something will inevitably shift. Just by experiencing what we are feeling we have taken the first step to resolution.*

The next step is to name what we are feeling because that helps us regain control and a little distance. Then as we give ourselves some time the solution invariably unfolds and becomes clearer. At that stage we are well on our way to resolving the situation. Often a night's sleep will enable us to see things differently. We gain a different perspective.

We won't necessarily resolve everything overnight; it can often take weeks, months or sometimes years. It is important to be gentle with yourself and know that you are holding a tension that could be projection - either your projection onto another or their projection onto you.

WHEN WE ARE TEMPORARILY OBSESSED

A quick jump to the neuroscience: when we ruminate about things too much, we risk becoming temporarily obsessed, lose our perspective, and fail to act logically.

David Rock[19] tells us that if we continue to think too much about a particular incident we risk overwhelming our limbic system and our brain does not work well.

We have to divert ourselves to do something else, go for a walk or work on something completely different, and when we come back to look at the problem it usually looks very different. We change our focus, refresh our brain, and free it from the lockdown of a particular mode of thinking.

When we start to obsess we have gone into a state of fear. We may not be aware of this on a conscious level but our crocodile brain is certainly aware and our level of cortisol, or stress hormone, has probably flooded our body. When cortisol is elevated our neo-cortex starts to shut down, waiting for the flight or fight reflex to kick in, so we are less able to think creatively. In fact, we are hardly thinking at all.

If we are able to sit in discomfort and self-reflect, we can take comfort in knowing that we are developing and changing our brain for the better.

Projection often plays a huge part in self-sabotage. When we notice ourselves obsessing, we are in self-sabotage mode. We need to notice what's happening, stop, and look objectively at what we are feeling and saying. We need to recognise that our behavior is coming from a much more primitive part of our brain and it is time to engage neo-cortex.

19   Dr David Rock, *Your Brain at Work.*

CHAPTER RECAP

- We all want to be loved, validated and looked after 24/7. Ideally, we would like our 3Ss met without any effort on our part. When we don't get that we feel disillusioned and project onto others.
- Projection is the oldest trick in the human armoury – it's not our fault; it is someone else's fault. Shifting blame and taking the focus off ourselves is human nature.
- Projection plays havoc with our relationships.
- Once we understand the concept we can become aware of when we are projecting by looking for emotional and physical triggers.
- Projection is not all negative. The positive qualities we see in others we also have, as long as we give ourselves permission to own them.
- Identifying our projections helps us understand our programming. And awareness of our projections is a valuable portal into our unconscious.
- When we feel emotionally reactive we have the opportunity to go deeper and learn more about ourselves. Knowing more gives us choice.
- Most of the time we are adept at using many different diversionary tactics to avoid attending to our own bodily signposts.
- What we resist persists.
- What we face dissipates.
- When we start to think obsessively we stop thinking creatively – in fact we aren't thinking at all!

YOUR JOURNEY

- In the exercises in the last chapter you thought about a person you disliked and perhaps were able to recognise that you had some ability to either recognise or act on some of those characteristics. Now let's consider the positive aspects of projection. Can you identify in yourself some of the traits that you admire in another?
- Can you identify situations where you have become emotionally reactive and work out what was triggered in you and why? (This is not about the other person and their actions. It is solely about you; which of your beliefs was impacted and what fear was your crocodile brain reacting to?)

CHAPTER 7

Projection

THE SEVENTH KEY

Our projections influence the way we think about others and that in turn affects our behavior.

- **Let's stop for a moment and do a brief recap.**
  Brain: 3 levels of the brain
  - Crocodile (manifests through the unconscious)
  - Horse (manifests through the unconscious)
  - Neo-cortex

  Unconscious:
  - What it does, how it works
  - How it is programmed
  - What happens when it feels threatened

  Beliefs:
  - Initially stem from programming of the unconscious by parents
  - Rarely changes in a lifetime unless underlying beliefs are examined
  - Largely accepted as the status quo

Secret Self:
- Represses so-called unattractive qualities
- Not acknowledged, nevertheless very human

Projection:
- The secret self's weapon
- The things we dislike or don't acknowledge in ourselves we see in others
- They then become our personal triggers
- Tells us about our unconscious beliefs and motivations

We know that projection is at play when we are emotionally triggered. If we can stop and think 'my secret self is trying to say something here, let's listen', this will cut the behavioral loop before we project outwards. This allows us to liberate trapped energy.

LIBERATING OUR ENERGY

It takes energy to protect our 'perfect façade.' It means we have to be continually aware of how we are coming across to others. It means that we are attempting to mind-read and often second-guess ourselves, which is tiring and time consuming. It also means we are not in the 'now' but in the past or future. **"Make the NOW the primary focus of your life,"**[20] says Tolle, because the present moment is all we have.

When we are in the past we are trying to work out how we came across, and if we are in the future we wonder how others will think, neither of which bodes well for sound relationships.

Successful interactions work best when we are fully in the moment, concentrating on the other. We connect, get resonance, and both parties feel seen and heard.

USING OUR SECRET SELF TO GAIN AWARENESS

Recognising our disowned secret self when we feel emotional distress or reactivity is a fundamental key to sustaining healthy relation-

---

20   Eckhart Tolle, *A New Earth: Awakening to your life's purpose.*

ships. When we take the time to reflect we gain self-awareness, enabling us to know ourselves better.

We begin to recognise some of our programming and check with ourselves whether it is OK or if we need a software update. Awareness gives us conscious choices, not choices springing from our unconscious wanting to protect our 3Ss. For instance, when we feel threatened many of us respond reactively by being devious, manipulative or dishonest etc. It is unlikely we would use those behaviors if we were making them in full consciousness.

Most of the time we want to disown our secret self. Rather than do this, start to welcome it as an invaluable tool for increasing your self-awareness. When we can see our own fallibilities clearly, even if we never act on them – e.g. I hate meanness and can see it like a flashing beacon in others yet acknowledge that at times I can be mean - we become slower to criticise others. When we are more self-aware we are aware of others and become slower to criticise and judge. We become more compassionate, understanding people, which can only be beneficial.

The biggest benefit occurs when we become less judgemental, more compassionate, and more understanding of ourselves. This enables us to relax more within ourselves and consequently we are more relaxed and loving with others.

Which, as the graphic to the right says, is very difficult but essential.

Throughout this book we have covered why and how our secret self has developed. We know it is fundamentally a protective tool, from an older part of our brain, and understand that unless it is brought into check, it can be extraordinarily destructive because unconsciously we usually want to find someone else to be the 'bad' guy. In crocodile terms we want to be the top crocodile or nearer the top than the bottom of the pecking order. The higher up the pecking order we are, we think we are safer and more secure, or at least better than other crocodiles.

I'm learning to
LOVE
MYSELF
it's the hardest thing I've ever done.

In your journey you are becoming aware that if you take the easy route and suppress discomfort as your preferred way of coping you only obtain short-term benefits. This strategy can and usually does sabotage relationships, and in the process deprives you of choice and empowerment. When we are unaware, we have limited choices, and our behavior springs from that primitive, unconscious, self-protective place which invariably finds another as a target.

You now have awareness and choice and already have turned a major corner towards happier, successful, satisfying relationships.

> *Dad comes home from work after a difficult day and stumbles over kids' toys at the front door. He yells at the kids to pick up their toys. Mum gets defensive; after all, the children are children and they have a right to play in their home.*
>
> *A few minutes later the eldest child is picking a fight with the youngest for being so messy and the youngest in frustration goes over to the sleeping cat and yanks her tail!*

Can you see the pattern? Can you see how the family are projecting their frustrations onto each other? First the father onto the children after his difficult day, then the eldest child blames the younger one, and finally projects his discomfort by plaguing the cat.

The scenario is familiar. Projection is at work; we all try to get rid of our anxiety and frustration somewhere.

> *Let's take that example further: Dad is yelling and Mum is getting defensive, thinking he's unreasonable. 'We are quietly getting on with life and he comes home with his bad mood and the contented energy in the house has just evaporated.' Later that evening Dad picking up Mum's vibe asks what's wrong and he gets met with a frosty comment 'nothing'. The rot has started, distance is established, Dad sulks and the situation goes from bad to worse. It is easy to see how these simple little projections have influenced the way Mum thought about Dad, and*

their behavior towards each other. This type of interaction erodes our relationships over time.

If Dad could have stopped himself yelling as soon as he walked in the door when he felt the anger rising, the situation could have been reversed – so easy to say, so difficult to do on the spur of the moment. However, for us, self-reflecting and recognising the opportunity for change, reactivity will be brought into check.

Let's continue to look at what is going on for Dad. His 3Ss had been triggered earlier in the day when his boss was dissatisfied with his work. As he walked in the door and saw the disorder in his home it unconsciously amplified his distress. When he was a child disorder in the house signalled the beginning of his parents' relationship breakdown. His mother was a 'neat freak' and when she became demotivated with her marriage she lost her impetus to keep the house ordered.

Gradually we start to see how all the little pieces add up to create a mosaic of emotions and triggers in our relationships.

Ideally Dad could have recognised the distress he was feeling and said to himself 'I am feeling a little vulnerable at the moment, I will be gentle with myself and reassure myself that things will be OK'. For her part Mum could have recognised the feeling of being criticised as being a trigger from her childhood and been less defensive. Later Dad may have worked out why his boss criticising his work worried him and would be in a better position to deal with the situation at work.

Quick recap: Our projections onto others influence the way we think about them, which in turn impacts our behavior and, like a chain reaction, then influences their behavior towards us.

THE NEUROSCIENCE

From a neuroscience standpoint we will always see situations through the lens of our own experience. We cannot fail because our experience and behavior has encoded our brain through the firing of neurons. Experiences shape neuronal connection through our memory. Encoding acts "as a kind of funnel,"[21] says Siegel, which we use to help us anticipate what is to come and prepare us for action.

The downside of seeing situations through the lens of our own experience is that this lens was formed out of conscious awareness, which unconsciously biases our perceptions and our view of reality. This subsequently impacts on how we engage with the world around us. It is frightening to realise that our programming is all happening out of our conscious awareness. An analogy may be someone altering the hard drive of your computer while you were out and you have no idea it's happened.

We know that ongoing experience continues to shape the brain throughout our life by altering the connections among neurons. As Siegel[22] says: "neural firing (experience) allows the brain to change its internal connections (memory). Experience shapes the brain and this process goes on throughout life ... we also know that the mind develops as the genetically programmed maturation of the brain responds to ongoing experience."

The interesting aspect is that while your interpretation of what you perceive is shaped by what you have experienced, your perception shapes how you process what you experience.

We have the ability to question and change our perceptions. This capacity to change perception is what gives us flexibility and brain plasticity.

IT MIGHT NOT BE US AT ALL BUT THEM

So far this has all been about us, but it is helpful to consider how all this information relates to other people. When others become reactive to us and we can't understand why, consider that maybe we are triggering something in their unconscious, which has nothing to do with us.

Others have their own programming and often, unbeknown to us, some aspect of our behavior or mannerisms may, at an unconscious level, remind them of someone else. Their association with that previous experience may have been unhappy and it triggered their crocodile brain into feeling aggressive or defensive. Conversely, it may have been a productive association, where someone was overly giving or

---

21   Dr. Dan Siegel, *The Developing Mind.*
22   Dr. Dan Siegel, *Pocket Guide to Interpersonal Neurobiology.*

attentive, and they unconsciously expect the same from us, which may be more than we are prepared or able to give.

> *Maria is a kind soul and lives next door to Cherie who is lonely and has few friends. Cherie's mother had been her primary companion but had recently died and since then Cherie is constantly coming over to spend time with Maria. It seemed that Cherie thought of Maria as a surrogate Mum, albeit unconsciously.*
>
> *This situation was wearing very thin with Maria, her own kids have all grown, left home, and she was relishing her own space. Cherie is completely unaware that she is projecting a mother figure onto Maria, and to start with Maria took on her projection with her kindly motherly caring.*
>
> *When she started to put firm boundaries around the time she spent with Cherie the relationship quickly turned very sour. Cherie was totally unaware of her projection and got angry and frustrated with Maria, accusing her of being a bad friend in a time of grief. Maria felt unappreciated, used, and angry. Both of them lost a friend and the comfort of having a great neighbour.*
>
> *What could Maria have done differently? Unless she had done what you are doing now, she probably could not have realised that Cherie was projecting a mother figure image on her. However, as she started to feel her frustration grow she could have talked to Cherie about needing her own time, there was a catch for Maria. She was unconsciously filling her own need to be caring. At some level she missed her mothering role with her own children gone.*

OTHERS ARE AT THE CENTRE OF THEIR OWN UNIVERSES; IT IS NOT ALL ABOUT US

When others become reactive and we can't understand why, it is helpful to stop and reflect. Others' anger either fuels our own anger or our defensiveness. This is a natural reaction and stems straight from our crocodile brain. It is important to take a step back before we react emotionally and expend precious energy, because it may not be about us at all.

When this situation arises in your relationships, check in with the other person to see if our actions have impacted them in some way. Ask questions such as: I feel something is going on for you, is it anything I have done or said? Or: I am concerned that I may have upset you in some way – is that the case?

We are so used to being the centre of our own universe we can find it extremely difficult to imagine that it is not about us at all. It is about the other person.

TAKING RESPONSIBILITY

At the end of the day, whether we like it or not, we are responsible for the choices and actions we take. You may be ordered to do something but ultimately you are responsible for the doing. No one can get into our head and physically manipulate or control our feelings. Responsibility for our relationships begins and ends with us.

We choose how we relate to everyone and everything in our life. We run our own control centre.

Sounds heavy doesn't it? The good news is that as we train ourselves to become aware we are changing our brain. We are using its plasticity to grow new neural connections and rewiring it for more positive behaviors, which sets us up for further successful interactions and rewarding relationships.

In the past our programming would have dominated the choices we made, but that was then and this is now. Now we are in a different place of awareness, a new state that befits us to reflect carefully when we catch ourselves resorting, for instance, to the old instinctive behavior of blaming others for the situation we are in.

It is difficult to take responsibility because we would prefer not to look at the part we play in our interpersonal relationships and circumstances, particularly when things are not working out the way we want. We don't want to admit our faults or own up to the part we have played. It is much easier to either become emotionally reactive or emotionally cut off than take responsibility. And we could blame our crocodile brain for that.

Responsibility means NOT demanding others to change their behavior so we feel better

Responsibility means not demanding others to change so that we feel less anxious, frustrated, upset, depressed, angry, victimised or whatever the emotion is. Responsibility is recognising what we are feeling and taking control of our emotions, not projecting them onto others.

> *Blake is a student enrolled in a course beyond his capability. Struggling, he complains the teaching is poor. It was easier to find fault and blame the teaching than to take responsibility for his part in choosing a course that was beyond his capability. He projected his own frustration by blaming the teacher.*

How often do we blame others when things go wrong? Whether it is our parents, our friends or our work mates.

Translating Blake's example into the work environment, most of the time we would rather change jobs than admit culpability for our part in a difficult dynamic with our boss or our peers. We often project onto them accusing them of being difficult. And indeed, they may be difficult, and usually are, but we have a part to play in this dynamic and we are also choosing to see them as difficult rather than think creatively about the situation. What can I learn to do differently? How can I look at this situation another way?

Remember each time we do something different we are establishing new neural connections improving our brain functioning.

CHAPTER RECAP

- Our projections influence the way we think about others and that in turn affects our behavior. It is a chain reaction.
- When we feel emotionally reactive our body is sending us a signal. This is our opportunity to stop and reflect.
- Ideally, we want to be gentle and compassionate with ourselves when we find ourselves judging others harshly, welcoming the opportunity to learn about our secret self and our reactive, instinctive crocodile brain, rather than trying to avoid or deny what we are feeling.
- In the same way others trigger us and our programming, we may be triggering them. Often this is at an unconscious level and it's not about us at all. If we can check out with them what is happening the relationship will grow.
- We are ALL 100% responsible for the thoughts and actions we take.
- We run our own control centre. No one else can get into our head and physically manipulate or control our feelings, so responsibility for all our relationships begins and ends with us. We choose how we relate to everyone and everything in our life.

YOUR JOURNEY

- Think of a situation in your personal life that impacted your interactions with others. How do you think others could have been influenced by your mood?
- Think of someone else that you find difficult and reflect on what might be happening in their personal life and how that might be impacting their behavior towards you.

CHAPTER 8

Impact on Relationships

What does this mean for your relationships?

The extraordinary scientist Albert Einstein told us "you cannot solve problems at the same level of consciousness that created them." And that is why it is important we learn different strategies if we want our relationships to function well.

We know that we can't advance to our full potential when the 3Ss are threatened, when survival mechanisms kick in effective listening goes out of the door and so do successful interactions. When the 3Ss are rampant we are very likely to self-sabotage without even realising it. We think and do things that ultimately work against us and we usually don't even realise it until later when our relationships deteriorate.

We know that arguing and disharmony leads to our own hardship and suffering.

We are all guilty of anger and frustration at times, after all we are human. Often the thoughts and beliefs that give rise to the angst are out of conscious awareness until we do this work.

As we know, to raise our level of awareness we need to become conscious of the power of our unconscious and the underlying motivations behind our thoughts and actions. Becoming responsible for

our thoughts and actions we maximise our potential to be flexible, innovative, and creative. Education as well as self-monitoring enables us to become empowered, valuable people who are not reacting out of a defensive 3 'S' state.

BEING OPEN

We cannot develop creative solutions to interpersonal problems unless we can hear, see, and open up to include the whole of who we are, our feelings, our personality, our history, and our desires.

Part of the new paradigm is to be open, which can feel vulnerable. Paradoxically, that vulnerability is our greatest strength. It allows us to become more real, honest, and authentic which brings greater energy with it. Our authentic self comes from a place of personal truth. Often it is our fear of being thought inadequate and vulnerable in some way that gets in the way of being open and being all of who we are. Openness means that our ideas can be challenged and rejected. They can even be thought of as stupid, which no doubt is what many of us heard throughout our childhood and at some level have probably absorbed as truth.

Fear of being considered incompetent is an almost universally held belief. Fear of foolishness closes us down and we assume others, know better. This cycle self-perpetuates, increasing the belief of inadequacy and locks us into fear – back to the 3 'S's. If we can override our own fear and reveal our ideas, we give others permission to come up with other ideas. They may not always be appropriate, yet often seed creativity, connection, as well as laughter. Perhaps more importantly disclosure will bring closeness and team spirit, giving rise to fertile ground for solving problems and interpersonal difficulties. We stop self-sabotaging.

WORKING AT A HIGHER LEVEL
OF CONSCIOUSNESS

When we take responsibility for instigating different behavior it has an automatic flow-on effect to others. This is because when one part of a system changes the whole system has to change. Imagine a clock, when one part doesn't work properly the clock can't function efficiently. The same applies to a car or any other system, and we are part of our own system of family and friends, within the greater systems of country and planet.

As people see us change little by little they change too. Whilst we can't change others (once they are no longer children) we can be role models by being respectful and responsible. We can support change by modelling it. We become more respectful and this helps to break the damaging 3S cycle. We start to work at a higher level of consciousness. Synergies flow and together we become greater than the sum of our parts.

We become empowered and can make rational choices for our highest good. This substantially reduces our stress levels, our reactivity to others, and our overall happiness, all major contributors to relationship success. Making our own choices of how to behave in any given situation gives us dignity. Our attitude is the full expression of who we are.

For the most part becoming conscious, responsible and authentic, disables old ingrained behavior patterns, learned as small children to avoid trouble when we felt helpless and powerless. After all, even Adam and Eve avoided responsibility by blaming the serpent!

Becoming responsible means, we are no longer operating out of our crocodile brain, we are operating at the highest level of our brain, our neo-cortex.

In becoming aware we know if we are operating out of love or fear. It really does come down to being that simple. A useful question to ask is, am I doing this out of love or fear? If the word love does not sound appropriate, we could replace it with respect or care for both yourself and others, which is essentially what love is. When we transcend the fear and our unconscious reactions (3Ss) and choose to respond from a place of respect, we are magnificently empowered. Empowerment gives us a feeling of choice, of strength of self-control, of being the best we can be.

CHAPTER RECAP

- Awareness of the power of our unconscious raises our level of consciousness.
- When we understand the negative 3S cycle our relationships can prosper.
- Being open allows us to become more real, honest, and authentic. Our authentic self comes from a place of personal truth.
- When we make rational choices for our highest good we reduce our stress levels, our reactivity to others and our overall happiness improves.
- We maximise our potential when we become responsible for our thoughts and actions. We no longer operate out of our crocodile brain we are working from the highest level of our brain.
- We reinvent and renew ourselves when we operate with intent, consciousness, authenticity, and attention.

YOUR JOURNEY

- Can you identify situations when you were too scared of what other people thought to be open and honest about what you thought or wanted?
- What was the impact on you, both long and short term?
- Can you see areas where there is the potential for you to let go of conditioning and be all of who you are?

CHAPTER 9

Empowerment - Our Reward

SEVEN KEYS

> 3 main points, awareness, choice,
> and responsibility

know this is not a good sales pitch but it's the truth. It's tough being responsible. It takes a lot of courage. Becoming responsible, honest, authentic, and conscious takes continual self-monitoring and discipline.

However, we reinvent and renew ourselves when we operate with intent, consciousness, authenticity, and attention." says Scharmer.[23] He has a "simple assumption: every human is not one but two. One is the person who we have become through the journey of the past. The other one is the dormant being of the future we could become through our forward journey. Who we become will depend on the choices we make and the actions we take now."

In Chapter 7, we looked at the first 5 keys to successful relationships. Now let's look at the last 2.

THE RELATIONSHIP

- Continually impacted by our projections and beliefs about how others should behave, which are largely unconscious

---

23   Dr. Otto Scharmer, *Theory U, Leading from the future as it emerges*, 2007.

- All the repressed and suppressed energy from our secret self and our beliefs find a home in others!
- Our personal triggers impact others, mainly negatively
- **RESULTS: DISASTROUS**

SOLUTION

- Understand your unconscious programming
- Take responsibility
- **RELATIONSHIPS: FLOURISH**

As you can see from the above and what we have already covered, when we take **responsibility for ourselves relationships flourish**, and the chance of self-sabotaging is greatly reduced. With a desire to really embed our learnings, here are the 7 keys again:

- Awareness of where our behavior originated
- An understanding of our programming and some of our personal drivers
- We know our programming manifests itself in our secret self and then in our behaviors
- We know we have a point of choice in how to behave in each and every interaction, without our unconscious making a quick almost automatic decision out of our awareness
- We know that when we have problems in our interpersonal relationships that it is often more about us and our programming than it is about other people
- With awareness we enable a more informed choice of action
- With this understanding we in turn realise that others may be unconsciously reacting out of their own programming and it may not have anything to do with us, which gives us the opportunity to defuse a potential conflict or not be as affected as we might once have been. Like us, they see the world through the lens of their own experiences.

We come from this:

To this:

AWARENESS

These seven principles distil into three key points:

- **Awareness** of where our behavior comes from
- **Knowledge** gives us choice in how we behave in each and every interaction
- **Responsibility** for our part in any interpersonal dynamic

We know that successful people are self-motivated and self-managed. In short, they are disciplined and responsible, as well as wanting the best for both themselves and others. They do not blame circumstances and other people; they work hard to find their way around difficulties. They fulfil commitments when they say they will. They know it takes continual discipline, self-monitoring, and determined courage in order to achieve. They also have the passion to be the best that they can be.

We all want to be successful people, and that will look different for each of us, but what we do know is that it is a hard continuous task. The payoffs for that difficult work are enormous. When you understand yourself better you automatically understand and appreciate the dilemmas that face others. You will read people more easily and effectively. You will be able to help and perhaps even guide them respectfully, without undue frustration in most cases. There will be exceptions and after giving others a fair opportunity for change, you will need to make a decision about whether you want them in your life.

Coming back to what we have learned by looking at both the psychology and neuroscience of how our brain works, we know that it is both remarkably primitive and sophisticated at the same time. Our brain is primed to look after itself and ensure survival, but it takes huge brain energy/effort to stop reacting, become more conscious and take responsibility. We know survival is hard-wired and its default patterns are firmly entrenched, but when we can fully grasp the principles above, it becomes so much easier to manage ourselves. While we are trying to be the best we can be, we have a brain that wants to dominate in the way it thinks best, and we need to harness its ability and use all of our attributes.

We need to harness our crocodile and our horse or mammalian brain - and be firmly in the saddle directing our lives.

We know that the brain changes when we focus, says famous psychiatrist and researcher Dr. Norman Doidge in his wonderful book, *The Brain That Changes Itself.*[24] Attention changes the brain if we pay enough attention to stimuli, but it is often difficult to direct that attention for long enough. The key is to hold the focus so new neural circuits grow and develop. As we focus on what is happening to us emotionally, we become more aware and can self-reflect. Over time, doing this regularly, we are lifting and enhancing our level of conscious. We are becoming more conscious. This focused self-reflection, as a conscious process, can deepen self-understanding. Taking time to reflect opens the door to conscious awareness bringing change. All of this leads us to a whole new level of consciousness and enables us to reach our fullest potential in every way.

---

24   Dr. Norman Doidge, *The Brain that changes itself.*

We have gained a new level of empowerment, and the more we can act on these key understandings the greater our impact. Everything gets easier – our lives, our relationships, our work, and finally our world.

THE GREATEST GIFT WE CAN GIVE OURSELVES AND THE PLANET

An Indian holy man once said that the greatest gift we can give the planet is a healthy you. This is undoubtedly true.
What is psychological health?

- Psychological health is an integration of yourself
- Acknowledging and embracing your secret self
- An ability to hold the tensions of competing demands and conflicting ideas with composure, knowing that we are trying to do the best we can
- An ability to take responsibility for yourself and your actions
- Communicating honestly with yourself and others
- Being aware of your projections
- Having a strong belief in yourself
- Most importantly having respect for yourself

When we can do all that, we are psychologically healthy and we know that our brain is changing accordingly – our flexibility translates as brain plasticity.

As a rule, when we are psychologically healthy, our biology follows suite. The neuroscience tells us that every time we feel an emotion our brain sends a chemical flush of hormones through our body. If those emotions are negative our body will receive a quick flush of cortisol (stress hormone), which as you can imagine is not good if it is happening often. While we are

becoming more and more aware, we are able to control those negative chemical flushes, and as we train our brains we are also changing our bodies. At the same time the flow-on is a better world with happier relationships. The greatest gift you can give yourself is an unconditional belief in yourself, and the greatest gift you can give the world is to become self-aware and take responsibility for your feelings and actions.

Your greatest gift to humanity, is a healthy you.

The Seven Keys To Empowerment

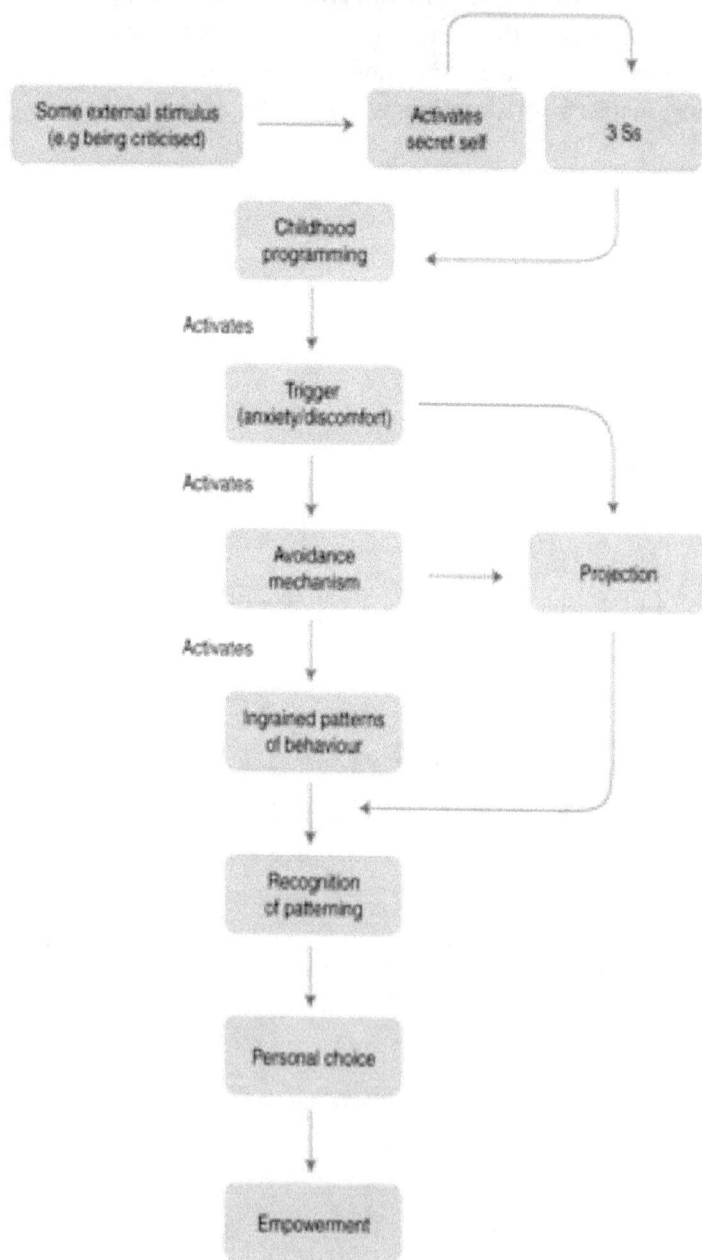

```
Some external stimulus          Activates
(e.g being criticised)  ──────▶  secret self          3 Ss
                                                        │
                                                        │
   Childhood  ◀───────────────────────────────────────┘
   programming
       │
  Activates │
       ▼
   Trigger ───────────────────────┐
 (anxiety/discomfort)              │
       │                           │
  Activates │                      │
       ▼                           ▼
   Avoidance  ─ ─ ─ ─ ─ ─▶     Projection
   mechanism                       │
       │                           │
  Activates │                      │
       ▼                           │
  Ingrained patterns               │
   of behaviour                    │
       │  ◀────────────────────────┘
       ▼
   Recognition
   of patterning
       │
       ▼
   Personal choice
       │
       ▼
   Empowerment
```

Brain
- 3 levels of the brain
- Crocodile (manifests through unconcious)
- Horse (manifests through unconscious)
- Neo-cortex

Uncon-cious
- Unconcious - What it does, how it works
- How it is programmed
- What happens when it feels threatened

Secret Self
- Secret self - repressed so-called unattractive qualities
- Not acknowledged, nevertheless very human

Beliefs
- Initially stem from programming of the unconcious by parents
- Rarely change in a lifetime unless beliefs are uncovered and examined
- Largely accepted as the status quo

Projection
- The secret self's weapon
- The things we dislike or don't acknowledge in ourselves we see in others
- Become our triggers
- Tell us about our unconcious beliefs and motivations

The Relation-ship
- Continually impacted by our projections and beliefs about how others should behave, which are largely unconcious
- All the repressed and the suppressed energy from our secret self and our beliefs find a home in others!
- Our personal triggers impact others, mainly negatively
- RESULT DISASTROUS

Solution
- Undestand your unconcious programming
- Take responsibility
- RELATIONSHIPS FLOURISH

ABOUT THE AUTHOR

From investment banking in both London and South Africa, as well as financial journalism, I found my passion and delight in psychotherapy. While my undergraduate degree is in French, I have a graduate diploma and Master's degree in psychotherapy.

Today I train therapists at Masters Level with the Jansen Newman Institute, work with the University of New South Wales Business School (AGSM) helping coach executives and I also have a private practice. I have worked and continue to work with many hundreds of people from different organi-sations – from people mandated by the courts to the heads of industry. I work extensively with women in women's empowerment programs.

The books I have written are:

- **You Can Live with Anyone, Well Almost,**
- **The Brain's Business – Psychology and Neuroscience for Exceptional Leadership**
- **Your Brain - Friend and Foe**

My passion is to help people understand why they think the way they do and fulfil their own highest potential. I believe that when we understand why we think as we do we have choice in how we choose to react. We are our own greatest saboteur and when we have an idea of how our brain works we can remove our own roadblocks and go from strength to strength.

Illustrations:
Rodrigo Adolfo

laurel@keeperconnections.com | www.thecogjameffect.com
Fighting Couple https://imonlyme.blog › 2019/03/06 › im-angry
Woman in chair https://tr.123rf.com/profile_evilratalex
Girl hands on hips https://www.gettyimages.com/illustrations/rude-child
Cute couple https://www.dreamstime.com/royalty-free-stock-image-cute-cartoon-couple-image1712086
Couple word bubble https://www.dreamstime.com/illustration/cartoon-friends-talking.html
Woman teaching child chair https://www.dreamstime.com/illustration/tutoring.html

ABOUT KHARIS PUBLISHING

Kharis Publishing is an independent, traditional publishing house with a core mission to publish impactful books, and channel proceeds into establishing mini-libraries or resource centers for orphanages in developing countries, so these kids will learn to read, dream, and grow. Every time you purchase a book from Kharis Publishing or partner as an author, you are helping give these kids an amazing opportunity to read, dream, and grow. Kharis Publishing is an imprint of Kharis Media LLC. Learn more at

www.kharispublishing.com

www.ingramcontent.com/pod-product-compliance
Lightning Source LLC
LaVergne TN
LVHW052035080426
835513LV00018B/2333